Innovation and Entrepreneurship

The effective management of innovation and entrepreneurship is vitally important for managers, organisations and governments. This concise textbook examines strategic approaches and concepts relevant for the effective management of innovation and entrepreneurship, supported by practical insights from a variety of industry sectors.

The book:

- Identifies the key challenges and dilemmas faced by managers and executives charged with leading, stimulating and sustaining innovation within large complex organisations.
- Explores the critical factors that drive entrepreneurial venture creation and growth, including the search for opportunities, the management of risk and the evaluation of alternative funding sources.
- Considers how innovation and entrepreneurship can be facilitated through the development of technology, knowledge, intellectual property and networks.

Each chapter includes an essential summary of the key points, a practical example focusing on innovation and entrepreneurship in action, discussion and reflection activities, as well as further reading suggestions.

Innovation and Entrepreneurship provides a practical and concise introduction for executive education students studying MSc and MBA apprenticeship programmes, as well as supplementary reading for postgraduate students studying modules on Innovation and Entrepreneurship.

Mike Kennard is Senior Lecturer in Innovation, Strategy and Entrepreneurship at Alliance Manchester Business School, University of Manchester, UK.

Management Practice Essentials

This series of Shortform textbooks has been developed to align with and support the Level 7 Senior Leader Master's Degree Apprenticeship (SLMDA). Each book concentrates on a key element of the SLMDA Standard and therefore covers a core essential of management practice. The series is centred around critical reflection on the underlying assumptions the individual leader or manager might make and their current practice, and collectively designed to enhance leadership knowledge, skills and behaviours. An ideal approach for any executive education course delivered through blended learning, and a useful alternative or supplement to traditional textbooks for a range of postgraduate Business & Management modules, the books:

- Combine theory and practice—providing students with knowledge and critical understanding of the theories, concepts and principles of leading organisations and focusing on the practical application and execution of these concepts.
- Are experience-led—providing students with the opportunity to develop their intellectual, practical and transferable skills and behaviours necessary to successfully analyse, develop and manage organisations.
- Include features to aid learning and understanding, such as chapter objectives, summaries, reflective questions and additional PowerPoint slides and cases available online.

Reflexive Leadership in Context
Paul Evans

Innovation and Entrepreneurship
Mike Kennard

For more information about the series, please visit www.routledge.com/Management-Practice-Essentials/book-series/MPE

Innovation and Entrepreneurship

Mike Kennard

LONDON AND NEW YORK

First published 2021
by Routledge
2 Park Square, Milton Park, Abingdon, Oxon OX14 4RN

and by Routledge
605 Third Avenue, New York, NY 10158

Routledge is an imprint of the Taylor & Francis Group, an informa business

© 2021 Mike Kennard

The right of Mike Kennard to be identified as author of this work has been asserted by him in accordance with sections 77 and 78 of the Copyright, Designs and Patents Act 1988.

All rights reserved. No part of this book may be reprinted or reproduced or utilised in any form or by any electronic, mechanical, or other means, now known or hereafter invented, including photocopying and recording, or in any information storage or retrieval system, without permission in writing from the publishers.

Trademark notice: Product or corporate names may be trademarks or registered trademarks, and are used only for identification and explanation without intent to infringe.

British Library Cataloguing-in-Publication Data
A catalogue record for this book is available from the British Library

Library of Congress Cataloging-in-Publication Data
Names: Kennard, Mike, 1971– author.
Title: Innovation and entrepreneurship / Mike Kennard.
Description: Abingdon, Oxon ; New York, NY : Routledge, 2022. | Series: Management practice essentials | Includes bibliographical references and index.
Subjects: LCSH: Technological innovations—Management. | Technological innovations—Economic aspects. | New products. | Creative ability in business. | Entrepreneurship.
Classification: LCC HD45 .K454 2022 (print) | LCC HD45 (ebook) | DDC 658.5/75—dc23
LC record available at https://lccn.loc.gov/2021006246
LC ebook record available at https://lccn.loc.gov/2021006247

ISBN: 978-0-367-51057-2 (hbk)
ISBN: 978-0-367-51058-9 (pbk)
ISBN: 978-1-003-05225-8 (ebk)

Typeset in Times New Roman
by Apex CoVantage, LLC

Contents

	About the author	vi
	Preface	vii
	Acknowledgements	ix
1	What are innovation and entrepreneurship?	1
2	Ideas, opportunities and creativity	13
3	New venture start-up and growth	26
4	Developing and sustaining innovative and entrepreneurial organisations	40
5	Knowledge Management, collaboration and User-Centred Innovation	52
6	Intellectual property and Open Innovation	63
7	Disruptive innovation and technology management	78
8	Strategic innovation management	91
	Further reading	105
	Index	108

About the author

Dr Mike Kennard is a Senior Lecturer in Innovation, Strategy and Entrepreneurship at Alliance Manchester Business School. Mike's teaching, research and consulting interests centre on innovation management capabilities, organisational barriers to innovation and developing entrepreneurial growth strategies.

Mike has worked with a wide range of organisations, including Airbus, Alliance Boots, Amey, Arriva, BAE Systems, General Electric, GKN, Intouch Group, KPMG, NHS, Northern Trains, Rolls-Royce and SABMiller. He is a regularly invited speaker on innovation, including events held by the Royal Aeronautical Society, Marketing Week, the International Society for Professional Innovation Management, the Institute of Materials, Greater Manchester Chamber of Commerce, and the Nottinghamshire Healthcare NHS Foundation Trust.

Previously Mike was Programme Director for the MSc Management and MSc Advanced Engineering Management programmes at the University of Birmingham, MBA Director at Aston Business School, and an Innovation Research Fellow at Nottingham University Business School. Mike also worked for over ten years in various management positions at Rolls-Royce plc, including Programme Manager for the Global Research and Technology Programme, and Programme Manager for the Trent 1000 Fan Module designed for the Boeing 787 Dreamliner.

Mike holds a first-class honours degree and PhD in engineering from the University of Birmingham, and an MBA from Nottingham University Business School. Mike is also a Chartered Engineer, Member of the Institute of Engineering and Technology, Member of the British Academy of Management, Senior Fellow of the Higher Education Academy and Distinguished Fellow of the Teaching Academy. Mike can be contacted via LinkedIn.

Preface

This book is concerned with understanding how organisations develop and manage innovation and entrepreneurship. The book explores the key theories that shape our understanding of innovation and entrepreneurship, supported with practical insights from a variety of different industry sectors.

Innovation and entrepreneurship are important to individuals, organisations and governments and significantly impact the economic development of nations. Innovation and entrepreneurship are not only part of new venture creation but also exist within established organisations operating in the private, public and social sectors. This book considers the need to understand innovation in terms of the creation of new combinations, new ways of doing things, new methods of production, new products and services and the formation of new ventures both inside and outside organisations.

The book systematically builds on key theories linked to these areas to develop a thorough understanding of the management of innovation and entrepreneurship. With an emphasis on real case analysis, the book blends theory and practitioner insights to inform effective management of innovation and entrepreneurship. The book takes a strategic level perspective, identifying and exploring the key characteristics of innovative and entrepreneurial organisations.

Aims

This book is divided into eight chapters, and aims to:

1 **Provide** a concise and holistic examination of the key principles underpinning the concepts of innovation and entrepreneurship, together with frameworks for critically understanding current and emergent practice.
2 **Explore** the critical factors that drive entrepreneurial venture creation and growth, including the search for opportunities, the management of risk and the evaluation of alternative funding sources.

3   **Identify** key challenges and dilemmas faced by managers and executives charged with leading, stimulating and sustaining innovation within large, complex organisations.
4   **Consider** how innovation and entrepreneurship can be facilitated through the development of technology, knowledge and intellectual property both internally and externally through collaboration and Open Innovation networks.
5   **Evaluate** the factors which underpin the effective strategic management of innovation within large, complex organisations and to provide opportunities for critical reflection through the development of focused cases and discussion activities.

As we progress through the book, the interrelation and linkages between the topics emerge, and a holistic appreciation of both the theory and practice of innovation and entrepreneurship is developed. The book concludes with suggested further reading in some additional areas of innovation and entrepreneurship research and practice.

Acknowledgements

I'd like to thank my colleagues, friends, family and the Routledge team for their help, support and guidance in writing this book. I'd also like to thank the many organisations I have worked with over the years that have helped shape and develop my own understanding of innovation and entrepreneurship. In particular, many thanks to Hugh Evans for supporting the development of the Primordial Radio case used in Chapter 3. Finally, I'd like to thank the 2,500 BSc, MSc, MBA and Executive Education students that I have had the opportunity to meet. They have supported my own reflective practice on how to effectively teach innovation and entrepreneurship, and I hope this book will support the learning of future students. But more importantly, I hope they can apply this learning to their careers and develop the innovative and entrepreneurial organisations and enterprises that will be vital to generate a prosperous and sustainable future.

1 What are innovation and entrepreneurship?

Essential summary

1. Innovation and entrepreneurship are closely interrelated concepts. Although there are no universally accepted definitions, the following are proposed for the purpose of this book:

    Innovation is the process that generates value through the creation, development and implementation of new ideas, technologies, products, services and business models.

    An entrepreneur is an individual who identifies an opportunity and undertakes to start and grow a new innovative venture to benefit from the opportunity.

    So, entrepreneurs are innovators, and innovators can be entrepreneurs.

2. One of the most influential scholars to shape the field of innovation and entrepreneurship is the Austrian economist Joseph Schumpeter, who developed two competing models. The Mark I model proposed that incumbent companies are under threat from new innovative firms through a process of 'creative destruction'. The Mark II model proposes that incumbent companies have the size and resources necessary to successfully innovate, and it is the newer, smaller firms that are at a competitive disadvantage. Empirical evidence suggests the two models may in fact be complementary.

3. Innovation and entrepreneurship drive economic growth. The seminal research of David Birch demonstrated that job creation in the United States is driven by small, innovative high-growth firms termed 'gazelles'. In contrast, large slow-growth firms that find it difficult to innovate, termed 'elephants', are vulnerable to new innovative competitors. This means innovation and entrepreneurship are crucial areas for both organisations and government policymakers.

Definitions of innovation and entrepreneurship

You will perhaps be unsurprised to learn that there are no universally accepted definitions of innovation and entrepreneurship in either the academic or practitioner communities.

From the academic perspective the continuous development, exploration and expansion of the field provides a rich literature of ideas, insights and arguments. In our field it is perfectly acceptable to have multiple (and sometimes opposing) views which are equally valid and valuable.

From the practitioner perspective innovation and entrepreneurship will mean different things to different organisations operating in different contexts. In my view this is positive, giving scope to shape definitions which resonate within the specific organisation.

Definitions of innovation

The origin of the word innovation comes from the Latin 'innovare', translated as 'to make something new'. This central theme of 'new' is core to definitions of innovation.

For example, the UK government define innovation as:

> *The successful exploitation of new ideas.*

The Organisation for Economic Co-operation and Development (OECD) define innovation as:

> *New products, business processes and changes that create wealth or social welfare.*

The noted scholar Professor Everett Rogers defines innovation as:

> *An idea, practice or object that is perceived as new.*

And Harvard Business School's Professor Scott Anthony offers the succinct:

> *Something different that has impact!*

For the purpose of this book I propose the following definition:

> *Innovation is the process that generates value through the creation, development, and implementation of new ideas, technologies, products, services and business models.*

What are innovation and entrepreneurship? 3

For commercial organisations value may be expressed in metrics such as increased market share, revenues, profit or shareholder returns. For public sector organisations value is focused on improved efficiency and enhanced service delivery.

Processes need to be managed, and therefore innovation is a management task. This can come as something of a surprise to many organisations. Some believe innovation is a mysterious phenomenon that occurs randomly as a series of 'light bulb' moments. Others believe innovation can be achieved by throwing copious amounts of money into a room full of boffins, coffee and whiteboards and then standing well back. A few organisations believe innovation is not required at all and instead focus on relentless cost-cutting. They then receive an unpleasant surprise when their customers eventually leave for innovative competitors who can better serve their needs.

To give a stark illustration of this, data from the Kauffman Foundation indicates that around 50% of Fortune 500 companies drop out of the index every ten years. Some failed, some merged, some were acquired, some were broken up and others simply failed to keep up with the required levels of growth to maintain their position—overtaken by new innovative competitors. What is clear is that despite their substantial advantages in the market the everlasting upward trajectory of success their directors and shareholders expected simply did not happen. It is primarily for this reason that innovation is a critical factor that needs to be actively managed by organisations.

Definitions of entrepreneurship

Where does entrepreneurship fit in? When we read or hear the word 'entrepreneur' we immediately think of individuals who have started and run successful businesses, such as Sir Richard Branson, Sir James Dyson, Steve Jobs, Mark Zuckerberg, Jeff Bezos, Elon Musk and the panel on Dragons Den. But providing an actual definition is much more difficult.

Professor Peter Kilby famously compared attempts to define entrepreneurs as hunting the elusive Heffalump in the Winnie the Pooh stories:

> *He has been hunted by many individuals using various trapping devices, but no one so far has succeeded in capturing him. All who claim to have caught sight of him report that he is enormous, but disagree on his particulars.*

The origin of the word entrepreneur comes from the French 'entreprende', translated as 'to undertake'. The word entrepreneur was first used in the 18th century by economist Richard Cantillon, who viewed an entrepreneur as a 'risk taker'. The French economist Jean-Baptiste Say later developed the word entrepreneur to mean 'adventurer' and 'one who undertakes an enterprise'. Since then various economic schools of thought have emerged, including the Austrian School, British School, German School and American School.

Entrepreneurs are not simply business owners; they utilise innovation to identify and exploit new opportunities. According to Peter Ducker innovation is 'the tool of the entrepreneur'. In this context a working definition we will use for this book is:

> *An entrepreneur is an individual who identifies an opportunity and undertakes to start and grow a new innovative venture to benefit from the opportunity.*

So, entrepreneurs are innovators, and innovators can also be entrepreneurs. In addition, managers and staff within an established business can operate with an entrepreneurial approach, identifying and developing new business opportunities. This is sometimes termed 'intrapreneurship' or 'corporate entrepreneurship'.

It is for these reasons the concepts of innovation and entrepreneurship are integrated within this book and are a vital management discipline, whether you want to start and grow a new business, develop new opportunities for an existing business, defend against competitive threats, improve public services or enhance sustainability and develop wider societal benefits.

Creative destruction: Schumpeterian perspectives on innovation and entrepreneurship

The Austrian economist Joseph Schumpeter is possibly the most influential figure in the development of our understanding of innovation and entrepreneurship. Schumpeter held a Professorship at the University of Bonn and emigrated to the United States before the onset of the Second World War to join Harvard University. Schumpeter proposed two models to demonstrate how innovation and entrepreneurship drive economic growth, his Mark I Model and then later a less influential (but still valid) Mark II model.

Mark I model

Schumpeter's Mark I model proposes that new firms emerge using innovation to disrupt markets and threaten the position of existing firms. These

What are innovation and entrepreneurship? 5

new firms are founded by entrepreneurs and compete not on price but by creating one of five sources of significant change:

- Introducing new products or making an improvement to an existing product.
- Creating new markets, particularly export markets in new territories.
- Securing new sources of raw materials or semi-manufactured goods.
- Developing new methods of production that have not yet been validated.
- Creating new types of industrial organisation, particularly if the new organisation leads to the formation of a monopoly.

Schumpeter's view of an entrepreneur is someone who has the ability, vision and determination to bring about these significant changes and threaten the viability of incumbent firms. In this respect entrepreneurs are different to business owners and salaried managers who undertake 'routine' work. Crucially, entrepreneurs use innovation to create change and disrupt markets.

Schumpeter envisioned what he describes as a cycle of 'creative destruction', where the creation of new entrepreneurial firms causes the destruction of established firms that can no longer compete. This cycle of creative destruction drives economic growth, although as more firms enter the market there will be a gradual erosion of profitability until the next wave of innovation occurs.

Creative destruction is sometimes referred to as 'waves of creative destruction', the 'winds of creative destruction' or 'Schumpeter's gale' ('Schumpeter's wind' not sounding quite right somehow).

Mark II model

And then he completely changed his mind! Schumpeter developed his Mark II model while a professor at Harvard University, arguing that it is in fact the large incumbent organisations that have the capabilities and resources required to drive innovation and economic growth, with small start-ups unlikely to be able to compete. In this model the entrepreneur is not someone who starts their own business but rather is an employee or manager of a large organisation that behaves in an entrepreneurial way, that is, by utilising innovation to drive change.

So which model is correct? I would suggest that they are in fact complementary. There are many examples of the Mark I model at work. For example, Apple, Microsoft, Google, Dell, Starbucks, Walmart, Facebook and Ryanair are all firms created by entrepreneurs that grew rapidly to disrupt existing markets. On the 'destruction' side of the equation large corporate failures include Nortel, Kodak, Texaco, Kmart, and MG Rover Group.

Yet there are many large organisations that have survived (and have in fact prospered) for decades, for example, General Electric, Boeing, Ford, Procter & Gamble, DuPont and Shell. What separates successful organisations from the failures is the ability to retain their entrepreneurial spirit and innovate. Effective innovation management is therefore a key capability for both new and incumbent firms.

Elephants, mice and gazelles: the economic impact of innovation and entrepreneurship

The term 'gazelles' was coined by the American academic David Birch. Birch was a physics student at Harvard in the 1960s who was forced to sit through an introduction to economics course, perhaps as a punishment. Here he was taught about the economist's rational world of perfect information where firms acted in an identical way to minimise costs and maximise benefits.

However, as the son of a businessman, Birch felt the perfect world of the economist did not square with his own experiences and set about using his physics training to study firms at the individual level (the atoms) and find out what was really going on. In the 18-year period between 1969 and 1987 Birch and his team studied 12 million businesses, accounting for around 90% of all private-sector employment in the United States. This Herculean effort yielded some startling results that even now underpin our understanding of entrepreneurship and significantly influence government policy.

Birch found that instead of firms behaving as a stable homogeneous group there is actually tremendous turbulence, chaos and variation beneath the aggregated data showing overall economic growth or decline. For example, Birch found that every year around 10% of businesses and jobs are lost. Or put another way, every five years, half of all businesses and jobs in the United States are lost and must therefore be replaced by new businesses.

But which types of business actually generate these jobs? To facilitate the analysis Birch segmented businesses into three distinct groups that he termed mice, elephants, and gazelles.

Mice: These are the very small businesses where the owners draw an income but are not looking to grow. Examples include shop keepers, garages, electricians, plumbers and self-employed freelancers.

Elephants: These are large companies and corporations with over 500 employees. Elephants have established products, services and customers and are looking to grow, but they typically find that growth is difficult.

Gazelles: These are new businesses that are small but are growing at a high rate due to their development of innovative technologies, products, services and business models. It is these gazelles which are the driver for new job creation.

Birch found that elephants are often locked into cost-cutting and employment reduction through downsizing, rightsizing, outsourcing or offshoring. For example, between 1980 and 1987, Fortune 500 companies laid off 3.1 million people. However, gazelles are focused on rapid growth by applying technology to create services that often have no physical product, such as software, finance, education, telecommunications, consulting, healthcare, insurance and asset management. Growth is fuelled by access to capital, skills, and export markets for these services. The net effect is that during the same 1980 to 1987 period the United States actually added 14 million new jobs to the economy despite the Fortune 500 cull.

Birch also proposed that there is an inherent entrepreneurial spirit in the United States that fuels the formation of gazelles. He cites a survey showing that 38% of men and 47% of women would want to run their own business if they could have their dream job, ahead of athlete, test pilot, novelist and photographer (and presumably also ahead of academic).

Birch contrasts this with the situation he perceives in Europe. For example, in Holland, less than 2% of university graduates ever work for a small or medium-sized business. In France, 500,000 jobs from large corporations were lost between 1975 and 1983, but only 50,000 new jobs were created from new businesses in the same period. The 2008 economic crisis left Europe with double-digit levels of unemployment, particularly youth unemployment in countries like Spain, Greece and Italy.

Implications for government policy

What factors can facilitate new venture creation and growth? Birch suggests that what is required is a fundamental shift from the notion of job security with a single employer (the soon-to-be-extinct 'job for life') to employment security based on the skills and mobility of the individual.

Put simply, businesses and nations cannot compete effectively in a dynamic, globalised market if they only have a static labour force. They must therefore foster highly skilled, highly flexible and innovative workers who do not have to rely on benevolent corporations or the state for employment. The development of this type of workforce requires an integrated set of government policies that span schools, further-education colleges, universities, incentives for training, infrastructure development (e.g. high-speed broadband internet) and immigration.

Governments should also be concerned with facilitating the start-up and growth of gazelle firms, for example, through the provision of grants, a taxation system that encourages risk-taking and investment and a start-up-friendly regulatory environment.

Implications for large organisations

Where does all of this leave the large organisations (the elephants), and why can't they do a better job of innovation and growth? After all, they have several major advantages over gazelles, including higher levels of capital, access to new capital, existing products and services, established customers and brand presence, talented employees (one hopes), plant and infrastructure and significant experience of the market dynamics.

In addition, large corporations tend to have a wide portfolio of products and services, so if a new product launch fails it is not usually terminal for the business. In contrast, most new businesses focus on developing a single product or service on which success or failure depends. This means that in theory large corporations should be in a stronger position to take risks with introducing new innovative products and services to market (which links into Schumpeter's Mark II model).

Research in this area (e.g. Freeman and Engel, 2007) suggests that several factors combine to reduce levels of innovation in large corporations, providing opportunities for agile and innovative gazelles to seize opportunities and market share. These include:

- Internal competition for budgets and resources, leading to political infighting between managers and which slows down decision-making.
- Incentive and reward structures focus on the sale of existing products and services, not the development of new products and services.
- High levels of risk avoidance, driven by the fear of being perceived to fail with a new innovative product or service.
- The fear that developing new innovative products and services would cannibalise the sales of existing product lines.
- The fear that developing new technologies might undermine the power base of managers who have forged their reputation with the development of the current technology.

It can be appreciated that these constraints don't apply to gazelle businesses, which are typically focused on doing one thing right and whose small size and simple structure facilitates rapid decision-making in response to market opportunities and threats. The challenge for gazelles is to maintain their innovative edge as they grow and avoid becoming the elephants of the future. The challenge for elephants is to reignite innovation and their entrepreneurial spirit.

Innovation and entrepreneurship in action: the Innovator's DNA

As innovation and entrepreneurship have taken on increased significance for organisations and governments there has been a corresponding increase in research seeking to develop our understanding of the field to inform both practice and policy. An important area of study has been to explore what makes some people want to become entrepreneurs. One approach has investigated the influence of intrinsic personality traits, characteristics and behaviours. For example, it has been suggested that entrepreneurs have a high degree of risk tolerance, a high need for achievement (nAch), a desire for autonomy, a belief that they can control the achievement of goals (locus of control), and higher-than-normal levels of creativity, intuition and opportunism. Some scholars have even suggested entrepreneurial behaviour is associated with negative characteristics such as low self-esteem, non-conformity and anxiety. A second area has investigated the influence of extrinsic factors. These may include level of education, gender, ethnicity, societal norms, a history of entrepreneurship within the family, or events such as redundancy acting as a catalyst for starting a business.

There has also been a significant degree of research aimed at extending this work to identify the characteristics and behaviours of innovators operating within an organisational setting. One particularly notable study was undertaken by Professors Jeffrey Dyer, Hal Gregersen and Clayton Christensen (2009), who set out to identify 'the Innovator's DNA'. Their research was based on extensive empirical data collection and analysis; a six-year study of 25 entrepreneurs and a survey of more than 3,000 executives and 500 individuals who had started innovative companies or invented new products. They concluded that there are five generic 'discovery skills' that innovative leaders exhibit.

Discovery skill 1: associating

Associating is the ability to successfully connect seemingly unrelated questions, problems or ideas from different fields. Our experience, knowledge and exposure to fresh inputs can trigger new associations, which in turn may lead to novel ideas. A practical implication of this is that innovation teams are likely to be more successful if they are diverse and multi-disciplinary, comprising people with different knowledge, skills and experience that can be combined.

Discovery skill 2: questioning

Innovative leaders constantly ask why, why not and what if questions to challenge assumptions and perceived wisdom. For example, Michael Dell asked why a computer cost five times as much as the sum of its individual components. From this he devised an innovative online business model that significantly reduced the cost of computers and launched his successful business.

Discovery skill 3: observing

Innovative leaders carefully, intentionally and consistently look for small behavioural details in areas such as the activities of customers, suppliers and competitors. These observations generate insights about new ways of doing things.

Discovery skill 4: experimenting

Innovative leaders are constantly testing new ideas with small-scale experiments to find out what works and what doesn't before scale-up and product launch. They encourage their staff to experiment and share the learning within the organisation, with an open culture that is tolerant of failure.

Discovery skill 5: networking

Innovative leaders go out of their way to meet people with different ideas and perspectives to their own knowledge domains. This includes visiting other countries and cultures; attending conferences and trade shows and mixing with entrepreneurs, academics, politicians and thinkers.

Are there limitations to what we can learn from studying successful entrepreneurs and innovators? The problem is that when we seek to understand what leads to high performance by studying high-performing individuals or organisations our data collection, analysis and interpretations can potentially become distorted by the high performance itself. For example, when we look at a commercially successful leader we tend to interpret their behaviours, traits and decisions as positive because we know that ultimately they were successful. This is an example of what Professor Phil Rosenzweig terms the 'halo effect'. If you want your organisation to be innovative and successful you can certainly gain useful insights from how others have led, but you must not follow uncritically. The challenge of management is to continuously develop your knowledge, experience and capabilities and to have the courage to find your own path.

Discussion and reflection activity

1 How should innovation and/or entrepreneurship be defined in the context of your own organisation?
2 Why are innovation and entrepreneurship crucial to economic growth?
3 What should the role of government be in supporting innovation and entrepreneurship?
4 What do you feel are the most important attributes that entrepreneurs and innovators require to succeed?
5 To what degree do you feel luck, chance and serendipity determine the likelihood of innovation and/or entrepreneurial success?
6 What practical steps could you take to become more innovative and entrepreneurial?

Recommended reading

Abernathy, W. J. and Clark, K. B. (1985). Innovation: Mapping the Winds of Creative Destruction. *Research Policy*, 14(1), 3–22.
Acs, Z. and Mueller, P. (2008). Employment Effects of Business Dynamics: Mice, Gazelles and Elephants. *Small Business Economics*, 30(1), 85–100.
Baregheh, A., Rowley, J. and Sambrook, S. (2009). Towards a Multidisciplinary Definition of Innovation. *Management Decision*, 47(8), 1323–1339.
Birch, D. L. (1989). Change, Innovation, and Job Generation. *Journal of Labor Research*, 10(1), 33–38.
Dolfsma, W. and van der Velde, G. (2014). Industry Innovativeness, Firm Size, and Entrepreneurship: Schumpeter Mark III? *Journal of Evolutionary Economics*, 24(4), 713–736.
Drucker, P. (1985). *Innovation and Entrepreneurship*. New York: Harper and Row.
Dyer, J. H., Gregersen, H. and Christensen, C. (2009). The Innovator's DNA. *Harvard Business Review*, 87(12), 60–67.
Freeman, J. and Engel, J. (2007). Models of Innovation: Start-Ups and Mature Corporations. *California Management Review*, 50(1), 94–119.
Henrekson, M. and Johansson, D. (2010). Gazelles as Job Creators: A Survey and Interpretation of the Evidence. *Small Business Economics*, 35(2), 227–244.
Hull, D. L., Bosley, J. J. and Udell, G. G. (1980). Renewing the Hunt for the Heffalump: Identifying Potential Entrepreneurs by Personality Characteristics. *Journal of Small Business*, 18, 11–18.
Minniti, M. (2008). The Role of Government Policy on Entrepreneurial Activity: Productive, Unproductive, or Destructive? *Entrepreneurship Theory and Practice*, 32(5), 779–790.
Rosenzweig, P. (2007). *The Halo Effect and Eight Other Business Delusions that Deceive Managers*. New York: Free Press.

Spencer, A., Kirchhoff, B. and White, C. (2008). Entrepreneurship, Innovation, and Wealth Distribution: The Essence of Creative Destruction. *International Small Business Journal*, 26(1), 9–26.

Strangler, D. and Arbesman, S. (2012). *What Does Fortune 500 Turnover Mean?* Kauffman Foundation. www.kauffman.org.

Xing, J. L. and Sharif, N. (2020). From Creative Destruction to Creative Appropriation: A Comprehensive Framework. *Research Policy*, 49(7). https://doi.org/10.1016/j.respol.2020.104060.

2 Ideas, opportunities and creativity

Essential summary

1   Utilising a systematic process for generating ideas is an effective way to deliver a steady stream of new innovations. One approach is to focus on searching for new opportunities within the business environment. Peter Drucker proposes seven potential sources of opportunity for organisations (and entrepreneurs) to explore:

    - Unexpected occurrences.
    - Incongruities.
    - Process needs.
    - Industry or market changes.
    - Demographic changes.
    - Changes in perception.
    - New knowledge.

2   Innovation and entrepreneurship can also be supported by developing organisations that foster creativity. This is typically difficult to achieve, particularly in large, established and complex organisations, but presents an opportunity to smaller, more agile entrepreneurial companies. Creativity can be thought of as a combination of expertise, problem-solving ability and motivation and is considered at individual, group and organisational levels. Organisational factors and management practices that can restrict creativity include:

    - Insufficient provision of resources, such as time, budget and the people required to support the development of a project.
    - High levels of risk aversion and intolerance to failure within the organisation, leading to new ideas being continuously rejected.
    - Lack of trust and open communication, for example, through the continuous changing of project goals and objectives or the imposition of unrealistic deadlines.

14 *Ideas, opportunities and creativity*

3   Research and Development (R&D) is an important source of new ideas and opportunities for industry sectors such as IT, automotive, pharmaceuticals, aerospace and electronics. From a governmental perspective R&D also supports the high-growth gazelle firms and generates the associated national economic benefits. Developing regional and national R&D-intensive industrial 'clusters' that facilitate innovation and entrepreneurship is therefore of particular interest to policymakers. Research in this area is underpinned by Michael Porter's 'diamond model' of national sources of competitive advantage. Examples of successful clusters include:

- Silicon Valley, California, United States (Technology).
- Route 128, Boston, United States (Technology).
- The Cambridge Cluster (or Silicon Fen), United Kingdom (Biotechnology and Computers).

Ideas and opportunities

There is a critical difference between waiting for ideas to happen and utilising a systematic process for generating ideas. If you place innovation at the heart of your business strategy for growth, then just waiting for ideas to happen is unlikely to deliver the results that the business (and its investors) hope for. Utilising a process for generating ideas is much more likely to deliver a steady stream of new innovations in a much more repeatable and predictable manner, providing a more stable platform for growth.

Over the last 50 years one of the most respected business thinkers has been the late Peter Drucker, the Austrian economist who emigrated to the United States and went on to become a leading academic and advisor to the Fortune 500. We came across Drucker in Chapter 1 as someone who viewed innovation and entrepreneurship as very tightly coupled concepts, with innovation viewed as "*the tool of the entrepreneur.*"

Drucker viewed innovation as a disciplined and systematic process, firmly believing in Thomas Edison's adage that success is 1% inspiration and 99% perspiration. According to Drucker, ideas (and from them innovation and new ventures) come from a conscious and purposeful search for opportunities.

He identified seven distinct sources of opportunity for organisations and entrepreneurs to explore: unexpected occurrences, incongruities, process needs, industry or market changes, demographic changes, changes in perception and new knowledge.

1 Unexpected occurrences

Unexpected occurrences are perhaps the easiest source of new opportunities. Consider the story of McDonald's, the global fast-food franchise. Back in the 1950s, Ray Kroc, the founder of McDonald's, was a sales representative for a manufacturer of commercial milkshake machines. He noticed that one restaurant was ordering more machines than any other. When he investigated he found that this restaurant was wearing through their machines at a faster rate than other outlets—an unexpected failure.

Now Kroc could have ignored this and just carried on selling milkshake machines. But he was curious and on further investigation discovered that the milkshake machines from this particular restaurant were wearing out because they were simply selling far more milkshakes than the norm—an unexpected success.

The restaurant was very popular, and Kroc discovered that they had a process-driven system for producing food of a highly consistent quality for a low price. Kroc realised this successful formula could be replicated, went into business with the restaurant owners and McDonald's was born.

Fast food may sound a bit low-tech for a book on innovation and entrepreneurship. But consider the story of Viagra, developed by the pharmaceutical giant Pfizer. Viagra was actually developed as a treatment for angina, a heart condition that constricts the vessels that supply the heart with blood. However, during extensive trials the Pfizer team noticed something unexpected; trial participants seemed rather reluctant to hand back unused pills to the researchers. How strange.

On closer investigation the researchers found that there was an interesting side effect trial participants had not previously mentioned: enhanced libido and sexual performance. With this new insight Viagra quickly became the leader in the market for erectile dysfunction, generating billions of dollars in revenues for Pfizer.

2 Incongruities

An incongruity is something that seems out of place or strange for a given situation or environment. Drucker argued that incongruities are rich opportunities for innovation if we can identify them. For example, in the first half of the 20th century the shipbuilding industry focused on making ships faster or more fuel efficient based on the assumption that these two factors drove the economics of the industry. However, the reality was that the major costs and inefficiencies were actually tied up in the idle time ships were moored in ports waiting for goods to be unloaded and loaded. By identifying the incongruity between the assumptions and the reality of ocean shipping economics, shipbuilders focused on designing container ships, dramatically reducing the time in port and turning ocean shipping into a major growth industry.

3 Process needs

A process need is simply a problem that may seem obvious but for which a solution has not yet been designed. If you have ever said, "*If only someone would invent a. . .*" this means you have identified a process need, and maybe you could develop a solution (and reap the reward). An example is the development of the 'cat's eye' that helps drivers see the road ahead at night by reflecting back car headlights.

Before the development of the cat's eye, roads would either be unlit and extremely dangerous at night or would need to have mains-powered street lighting, which was extremely expensive to install on all the road networks, especially in rural areas. The cat's eye solved this process need; how to significantly improve road safety at night affordably. The British inventor of the cat's eye, Percy Shaw, patented his design, which then went on to be widely adopted around the world.

4 Industry and market changes

Industry structures and markets often change very quickly. The catalysts for change can be rapid industry growth or changes in legal or regulatory requirements. When industry or market changes occur, there are big opportunities for innovators and entrepreneurs to exploit the change. This opportunity is often strengthened because typically incumbent firms can be slow to anticipate change or react to change when it occurs, focusing instead on defending what they already have.

Examples of industry change include deregulation of financial markets, privatisation of nationalised industries, such as energy and water, and Open Skies, the name given to the liberalisation of the regulations governing the international commercial aviation industry.

5 Demographic changes

Demographic change opens up a multitude of opportunities for sharp-eyed innovators and entrepreneurs. Demographic changes affecting industrialised nations include growing populations, ageing populations, increasing affluence, migration and skills shortages.

Often the combination of demographic trends can amplify opportunities. For example, ageing populations combined with increasing affluence has led to the emergence of wealthy retirees who have high levels of disposable income, the so-called grey pound/euro/dollar.

Businesses that can offer new services and products to this demographic are likely to be successful. Similarly, an ageing and growing population provides numerous opportunities in the healthcare sector for entrepreneurs that can spot a gap in the market for new innovative products and services.

6 Changes in perception

Perceptions of the same phenomena can be vastly different, and identifying changes in perception can open up opportunities. For example, retired people once perceived that their retirement would be fairly sedate, perhaps involving some gardening and visiting the grandchildren once in a while. However, in recent years the perception of retirement has shifted to a much more active lifestyle involving travel and fitness—presenting opportunities for new businesses serving this market.

Another example concerns the perception of food. Many consumers still like to reduce their weekly shopping bill, as evidenced by the rise of discount grocers such as Aldi and Lidl. However, certain shoppers are actually prepared to pay more for food that they perceive has superior nutritional value or ethical credentials (or both). This has driven the rise in demand for organic fruit and vegetables and for ethically sourced Fairtrade goods, such as chocolate and coffee, both sold at a price premium.

7 New knowledge

Perhaps the best-known innovations have been developed as a result of new knowledge. These innovations are often the result of many years' investment in research but have the potential to be transformational. Historical examples include the printing press, the steam engine, electricity, the silicon chip and the internet. Three key areas of technology leading to the development of new innovations and new businesses are materials, biotechnology and information technology (IT).

However, it is important to note that new technology in itself is not innovation; it is the application and commercialisation of new technology that is innovation. For example, the recent discovery of the 'super-material' graphene by researchers at the University of Manchester is of limited use. It is the application of graphene's unique mechanical and conductive properties that will deliver new innovative products.

Fostering creativity

If Drucker emphasises a disciplined and systematic approach to generating ideas, then a useful counterweight is the research focusing on how organisational factors, such as culture, can facilitate a creative environment where ideas and innovation can flourish. This can be particularly difficult for large complex organisations focused on serving existing customers, improving productivity and controlling costs. Indeed some researchers have argued that it is more likely that large organisations unintentionally kill creativity than support it. Conversely, this presents an opportunity for smaller, more agile and entrepreneurial firms to succeed through developing an organisation that fosters high levels of creativity.

Individual creativity

When we think of the word 'creativity' it is often talented individuals from the arts which spring to mind, for example, famous artists, musicians and writers. A substantial amount of neuro-psychological research has developed our understanding of what makes people creative. Perhaps the most well-known model is the left brain/right brain theory, which won Roger Sperry the Nobel Prize for Physiology and Medicine in 1981. This proposed that the left hemisphere of the brain focuses on processing information in a narrow, logical and systematic manner. The right hemisphere supports thinking in a much more intuitive, unconventional and lateral manner and is therefore utilised more in tasks requiring creativity.

Within a business context this can often have the unfortunate consequence that some people simply feel they are not inherently creative and that therefore this should be left to others. But to be successful, businesses need to support and foster creativity in all of their employees. A useful way to consider individual creativity is that it consists of the interlinkage of three separate components: expertise, problem-solving ability and motivation.

Expertise: This is the combination of knowledge, technical skills and experience that an individual has built up over time through formal education, training and work. Individuals who have acquired a high level of expertise are able to utilise this to develop creative solutions.

Problem-solving ability: Individuals with well-developed problem-solving ability are likely to be much more flexible, curious and imaginative when they approach difficult problems, utilising the right side of the brain.

Motivation: This determines how likely an individual is to want to utilise their expertise and problem-solving ability to develop creative solutions. There are two distinct types of motivation to consider. Extrinsic motivation comes from external sources, for example, monetary rewards such as a bonus or pay rise. Intrinsic motivation is where the individual derives an internal sense of satisfaction from the act of working on an interesting and challenging creative task.

Group creativity

Most tasks within organisations are conducted not by individuals but by groups or teams of employees. The composition and operation of these teams is of critical importance for tasks which require creativity. Teams which are diverse and interdisciplinary are likely to be more successful than teams with a homogenous composition.

For example, a team of ten engineers will certainly come up with a sound design for a new product. However, an interdisciplinary team which includes staff from engineering, manufacturing, marketing, procurement and commercial functions is likely to produce a superior solution by drawing on a wider set of knowledge, experience, insights and perspectives.

Effective teams also need high levels of intrinsic motivation, high levels of trust and open communication. There also needs to be an environment where differing opinions within the team are heard and respected to avoid conformity, conflict-avoidance and 'groupthink'. This can restrict the generation and exploration of creative ideas.

Organisational creativity

Understanding the components of individual and group creativity is important because organisations can use it to develop structures, cultures and practices which support these. For example, expertise can be developed by hiring well-qualified people and then offering further educational, training and development opportunities. Evaluating an individual's problem-solving ability can form part of the recruitment and selection processes and can be further developed by providing training in techniques such as brainstorming, forced associations and root cause analysis. Extrinsic motivation could be provided through bonuses, pay rises, promotional opportunities, share options and profit share schemes. While intrinsic motivation comes from within the individual, organisations need to be mindful of inadvertently diminishing this through poor management practices. Some researchers (e.g. Amabile, 1998) suggest that a reduction in employee intrinsic motivation is the most common way creativity is killed within organisations. Organisational factors and management practices that can cause this include:

- Insufficient provision of resources, such as time, budget and the people required to support the development of a project.

- High levels of risk aversion and intolerance to failure within the organisation, leading to new ideas being continuously rejected.
- Lack of trust and open communication, for example, through the continuous changing of project goals and objectives or the imposition of unrealistic deadlines.
- Hierarchical, bureaucratic and rigid organisational structures and practices which inhibit freedom and autonomy and slow down decision-making.
- A general lack of support, encouragement and interest from managers.
- Autocratic and controlling management styles.
- Continual assessment and evaluation of the performance and outputs of creative individuals, teams and projects.

Managers should be mindful of these pitfalls if they wish to support and improve creativity within the organisation. They should also provide opportunities for employees to develop their capacity for creativity. There are many ways this could be achieved. For example, education and training, attendance at conferences and trade shows, opportunities to develop professional qualifications, internal secondments to broaden experience and perhaps external secondments so employees can benefit from experiencing how other organisations operate. In addition, provision of development opportunities is likely to be viewed as a form of reward and recognition, supporting high levels of intrinsic motivation.

R&D, clusters and innovation

Research and Development (R&D) is an important source of new ideas and opportunities for industry sectors such as IT, automotive, pharmaceuticals, aerospace and electronics. The advancement of new knowledge, scientific discoveries and technologies underpins the development of new products to meet current and future customer needs. From a governmental perspective R&D also supports the high-growth gazelle firms discussed in Chapter 1 and generates the associated economic benefits. A particular focus has been on developing research-intensive regional and national 'clusters' that support innovation and entrepreneurship.

Perhaps the most well-known and successful cluster is Silicon Valley. Located in the Santa Clara area of Northern California, Silicon Valley has become the home of some of the world's largest high-technology companies, including Apple, Cisco, Facebook, Google, Hewlett-Packard, Intel and Oracle, along with countless mid-sized companies and entrepreneurial start-ups. On first inspection it seems the companies in Silicon Valley have

Ideas, opportunities and creativity 21

become successful due to their ability to innovate by bringing new technologies and business models rapidly to market. But does the high density of firms within the same sector and geographic location itself play an active role in facilitating innovation?

The area is home to several excellent universities, for example, Stanford University, California Institute of Technology, University of California Berkeley and Carnegie Mellon University. These institutions all deliver a steady stream of research outputs and eager science, technology, engineering and business graduates into the local economy. The area also attracts venture capitalists keen to invest in start-ups that may become the next Apple, the next Amazon, the next Google and the next Facebook. A strong service industry has also developed to support business, for example, law firms specialising in areas such as intellectual property, initial public offerings (IPOs) and tax advice.

So, clearly a combination of factors have interacted and contributed to Silicon Valley's success, but can the precise nature of these interactions be sufficiently well understood and quantified to enable similar clusters to be developed elsewhere? Research into clusters (or 'industrial districts') has been performed since the 1920s. However, it was the publication of Harvard Professor Michael Porter's 1990 book *The Competitive Advantage of Nations* that sparked a rapid increase of research into the field.

Porter is best known for his work on firm competitiveness, and in particular his 'five forces' model and the concept of 'competitive advantage'. It was perhaps a logical step to see if this could be extended to a national level. In essence, firms compete against each other, and with the advent of globalisation, so do nations. Firms and nations that implement policies which generate a competitive advantage over their rivals will be successful; those who don't will end up like Kodak or Greece.

Porter looked closely at why particular industries became successful in certain locations, defining these clusters as:

> *Geographic concentrations of interconnected companies and institutions in a particular field.*

Porter proposed a 'diamond' model of four broad, interrelated elements to help explain the sources of national competitive advantage and the formation of clusters:

- **Factor conditions:** These include R&D, human capital, knowledge, plant, finance and infrastructure that are specific to an industry and drive competitiveness.

22   Ideas, opportunities and creativity

- **Demand conditions:** The size of the domestic market for improved products and services drives innovation and early sales momentum prior to establishing export markets.
- **Related and supporting industries:** These are mutually reinforcing, driving innovation and economies of scope. Examples include computer hardware and software, financial services and legal services, oil refining and plastics manufacturing.
- **Firm strategy, rivalry and industry structure:** A high degree of domestic firm rivalry and competition can drive innovation and raise the overall competitiveness of the cluster.

So, if Porter's diamond was applied to Silicon Valley a positive picture would emerge. Factor conditions are favourable, particularly with the human capital (graduates) and knowledge (research outputs) emanating from the university infrastructure and access to venture capital finance. Demand conditions are also high, due to the large population and wealth of the United States. Related and supporting industries are high, for example, hardware, software and legal services. Finally inter-firm rivalry is also high, for example, between Apple and Google in the smartphone market, which drives innovation in the functionality and utility of smartphone operating systems.

In addition to these four elements, Porter also acknowledges the role of government. For example, an early boost for high-technology firms based in Silicon Valley came from high levels of government defence research spending in the 1960s and 1970s, fuelled by the Cold War. Other examples of clusters include:

- Route 128, Boston, United States (High Technology).
- The Cambridge Cluster or 'Silicon Fen', United Kingdom (Biotech & Computers).
- Bangalore, India (Software Outsourcing).
- City of London, United Kingdom (Financial Services).
- Hollywood, United States (Film & Media).
- Aerospace Valley, Toulouse, France (Aerospace).
- Tech City, London, United Kingdom (High Technology).
- Milan, Italy (High Fashion).

Can a cluster actually be created as opposed to naturally evolving over time? Certainly governments have attempted to create clusters, and according to the 2007 Economist article 'The Fading Lustre of Clusters', billions of pounds, euros and dollars have been carefully invested using the following process:

Typically governments pick a promising part of their country, ideally with a big university nearby, and provide a pot full of money that is meant to kick-start entrepreneurship under the guiding hand of benevolent bureaucrats. This has been an abysmal failure—it is companies, not regions that are competitive.

However, it is important to recognise that clusters can be successful at facilitating innovation in R&D-intensive industry sectors. The earlier note of caution regards both the desirability and effectiveness of state intervention to promote innovation and entrepreneurship, a theme explored further in Chapter 5.

Innovation and entrepreneurship in action: WL Gore

In 1958 Wilbert Lee 'Bill' Gore turned his back on a 17-year career as an R&D manager at the chemical giant DuPont and founded WL Gore and Associates (henceforth WL Gore). What followed is pretty close to the archetypal American dream, where a business which started out in the family basement became a billion-dollar company operating in over 25 countries.

WL Gore's breakthrough innovation was the development of 'Gore-Tex', the patented breathable polytetrafluorethylene (PTFE) fabric. Today WL Gore has a worldwide reputation for bringing innovative products to markets as diverse as medical supplies, filters, guitar strings, dental floss and electrical components. But behind these products is the unique way in which WL Gore manages creativity and innovation. Bill Gore clearly formed a strong opinion on what he felt worked (and what didn't work) in terms of organisational design based on his experience at DuPont. When he founded his own company he effectively threw away the rulebook on how companies should be run and set up a unique and innovative business.

To start with there are no employees, only 'associates' who each own a stake in the business. There are no job titles, no hierarchy and no managers. New associates are assigned a sponsor and encouraged to find a project in which they are interested and start working on it. Leaders are simply people who can convince other people to follow them on a new project. Annual pay rises for associates are set by their peers and based on their individual and team contribution.

Recruitment is a lengthy affair, and appointment decisions are ultimately made by fellow associates. If a division rises above 200 associates, it is split up to retain a small-company feel. The company has core values of fairness, freedom, consultation and keeping commitments. In some ways the company feels like a giant social experiment—but does it work?

Well, WL Gore clearly have developed highly innovative products and have grown from nothing to a billion-dollar turnover company. In addition, the company is routinely voted as one of the best places to work in the countries in which it operates. Can this organisational system be copied by other companies? Not unless they are in the start-up phase, according to Bill Gore. Any larger established company would not be able to impose the culture change required.

Are there disadvantages? It is difficult to find much negativity or criticism of WL Gore in the literature or press. But by utilising this unique organisational system WL Gore may be limiting the talent pool of potential employees. Some people are uncomfortable with ambiguity, they like knowing who their boss is and what their job title is and don't want their pay set by their colleagues. But WL Gore are willing to accept this potential disadvantage in return for their organisational system, which fosters creativity, supports innovation and leads to the development of new products and revenue streams.

Discussion and reflection activity

1 Apply Drucker's opportunity framework to your organisation. What are the potential opportunities that emerge?
2 How creative do you feel you are as an individual? What steps could be taken to develop your individual creativity?
3 How creative do you feel your organisation is? What steps could be taken to develop creativity within your organisation?
4 What are the linkages between individual creativity and the five 'discovery skills' proposed in the Innovator's DNA (Chapter 1)?
5 Should governments support the formation and development of R&D-intensive regional and national clusters? How else could governments support innovation and entrepreneurship?
6 Would you enjoy working in an organisational system similar to WL Gore? What aspects of the WL Gore system could work successfully in your current organisation?

Recommended reading

Alvarez, S. and Barney, J. (2007). Discovery and Creation: Alternative Theories of Entrepreneurial Action. *Strategic Entrepreneurship Journal*, 1, 11–26.
Amabile, T. (1998). How to Kill Creativity. *Harvard Business Review*, 76(5), 76–87.
Anderson, N., Potocnik, K. and Zhou, J. (2014). Innovation and Creativity in Organisations: A State-of-the-Science Review and Prospective Commentary. *Journal of Management*, 40, 1297–1333.

Bjork, J., Boccardelli, P. and Magnusson, M. (2010). Ideation Capabilities for Continuous Innovation. *Creativity and Innovation Management*, 19(4), 385–396.

Cai, W., Lysova, E. I., Khapova, S. N. and Bossink, B. A. (2019). Does Entrepreneurial Leadership Foster Creativity Among Employees and Teams? The Mediating Role of Creative Efficacy Beliefs. *Journal of Business and Psychology*, 34, 203–217.

Catmull, E. (2008). How Pixar Fosters Collective Creativity. *Harvard Business Review*, 86(9), 65–72.

Drucker, P. (2002). The Discipline of Innovation, *Harvard Business Review*, 80(8), 95–103.

Eisingerich, A., Falck, O., Heblich, S. and Kretschmer, T. (2012). Firm Innovativeness Across Cluster Types. *Industry and Innovation*, 19(3), 233–248.

Engle, J. S. and del-Palacio, I. (2011). Global Clusters of Innovation: The Case of Israel and Silicon Valley. *California Management Review*, 53(2), 27–49.

Granstrand, O. and Holgersson, M. (2020). Innovation Ecosystems: A Conceptual Review and a New Definition. *Technovation*, 90–91. https://doi.org/10.1016/j.technovation.2019.102098.

Hamel, G. (1999). Bringing Silicon Valley Inside. *Harvard Business Review*, 77(5), 70–84.

Lazarow, A. (2020). Beyond Silicon Valley: How Start-Ups Succeed in Unlikely Places. *Harvard Business Review*, 98(2), 126–133.

Martins, E. and Terblanche, F. (2003). Building Organisational Culture that Stimulates Creativity and Innovation. *European Journal of Innovation Management*, 6(1), 64–74.

Porter, M. E. (1998). Clusters and the New Economies of Competition. *Harvard Business Review*, 76(6), 77–90.

Somech, A. and Drach-Zahavy, A. (2013). Translating Team Creativity to Innovation Implementation: The Role of Team Composition and Climate for Innovation. *Journal of Management*, 39(3), 684–708.

3 New venture start-up and growth

Essential summary

1 Entrepreneurs need to acquire funding that will support growth and the achievement of business goals. They need to consider whether the funding needs to be paid back, whether interest repayments are required and whether they will be required to give up an equity stake in their business. Funding options include:

- Grants.
- Family, friends (and fools).
- Personal savings.
- Loans.
- Angel investors.
- Venture capitalists.
- Crowdfunding.

2 Entrepreneurs need to consider resource constraints and the management of risk and radical innovation to drive growth. Resource constraints may include funding, infrastructure, labour or specialist skills and capabilities. Entrepreneurs can overcome resource restraints by employing a 'bricolage' approach of making best use of the resources at hand, often recombining them in innovative ways that in themselves can provide new opportunities to the firm.

Most innovations are 'incremental' and low risk in nature. Greater payoffs can be achieved by investing in higher risk 'radical innovation', which deliver greater improvements, are much more difficult for competitors to copy and can potentially deliver a sustained market-leading position. Entrepreneurial firms that adopt a radical innovation approach can therefore offer superior and differentiated products and services compared with established firms that are locked into incremental innovation.

3   Many established businesses use 'corporate venturing' to launch new ventures, reignite entrepreneurship and kick-start growth. Well-known companies that have introduced venturing programmes include Adobe, Intel, Lucent, Unilever, Procter & Gamble, Siemens, 3M and Xerox. Universities also 'spin-off' new ventures based on their scientific research and intellectual property. Corporate venturing generally takes one of three forms:

- Internal corporate venturing (ICV).
- External corporate venturing (ECV).
- Corporate venture capital (CVC).

Corporate venturing provides an effective mechanism to escape the constraints of the core business and explore new opportunities that will sustain innovation, entrepreneurism and growth.

Funding options for start-ups

New venture formation invariably requires funding, and the level of funding will vary depending on the nature of the business. Service-based businesses, such as consulting, may require relatively low levels of funding. Manufacturing businesses which require factories, machines and materials as well as labour will require higher levels of funding. Companies that are developing new technology and require research facilities and highly skilled labour will also require higher levels of funding.

Before launching a new venture it is prudent to write a business plan which details the funding required, what it will be spent on, and the point at which the venture will break even and become profitable. Business plans can vary from concise one-page summaries to lengthy, complex documents. Another consideration will be the legal structure of your business, for example, sole trader, limited company or partnership. Access to funding is a crucial factor, and entrepreneurs looking to fund a new venture have seven broad options:

1 Grants

Grants to support start-ups are often available from charities, local government or central government. Grants are usually very specifically targeted, for example, for types of entrepreneur (young, unemployed, disadvantaged), region specific, or industry sector specific. The government's Business Finance Support Finder directory lists over 300 direct grant agencies. The central advantage of grants is that the money is not paid back. The disadvantages are the restricted eligibility and protracted application process, with no guarantee of being awarded the grant at the end of it. Most grants are also for relatively small amounts.

2 Family, friends (and fools)

You may be able to access money from family and friends. How much and on what terms depends on your business proposition, strength of relationship and the financial means available. Sometimes the funding will be like a grant and is not paid back, and sometimes it will be a loan paid back with or without interest. It is recommended that the terms are agreed upon and recorded to avoid any future disputes. The term 'fools' alludes to the fact that many start-ups go out of business within the first three years, so lending money for a start-up is high risk and can lead to strained and damaged personal relationships in the event of business failure.

3 Personal savings

You could use your own personal savings to fund your start-up. You might build this up over time, release equity built up in your home, use money from redundancy or severance, or if you are retired but active you may take money from a pension lump sum. The advantage of using your own money is that there are no forms to fill in, you can spend it how you like, and you retain 100% ownership of your business. The disadvantage is that if your business fails you lose your investment.

4 Loans

The advantage of a loan is that you retain 100% ownership of your business. The loan will of course need to be paid back, with interest. High street banks are generally cautious when it comes to loaning money to start-ups. This caution comes from the aforementioned high failure rate of start-ups, and banks are therefore likely to charge a high interest rate to reflect the risk they are taking. For larger amounts they are also likely to ask for the loan to be secured against an asset, such as your house. If your business fails and you cannot repay the loan, the bank would repossess your house, even if your business had a limited liability structure.

Bank loans are therefore not to be undertaken lightly, and entrepreneurs should review several banks to ensure they are getting the most favourable terms. As well as traditional high street banks, entrepreneurs should also consider specialist business banks, not-for-profit agencies and government agencies that offer loans for start-ups at competitive interest rates, for example, startuploans.co.uk, startupdirect.co.uk, fundingcircle.com and virginstartup.co.uk.

5 Angel investors

Angel investors are wealthy individuals, usually with a successful track record in business, who invest in start-up or early-stage firms in exchange for an equity stake. Angel investors want the business to grow rapidly, therefore their equity stake will increase in value. Perhaps the most well-known example of angel investors in the UK are the 'dragons' in the BBC's *Dragons' Den* programme.

The advantage for the entrepreneur is that the money does not need to be paid back, even if the business fails. In addition the entrepreneur may benefit from the advice and support of the angel investor (who can act in a mentoring capacity) and may also gain access to the angel investor's contacts and network. The combination of these resources can facilitate rapid growth of the business.

Angel investors tend to have a wide variety of opportunities to invest in, so entrepreneurs must work hard to convince the angel to invest in them, usually through a compelling 'pitch' of their business idea. The other main disadvantage is that the entrepreneur will have to give up some of the equity of the business, which might have a substantial future value should the business become successful and grow rapidly.

6 Venture capitalists

Venture capitalists operate in a similar way to angel investors but are investment firms rather than individuals. Like angel investors venture capitalists will invest money in the business in return for an equity stake. Venture capitalists are likely to want to have a place on the board of the company and will have a much more hands-on input to managing the business.

Businesses that access venture capital funding will be aiming to achieve rapid growth, and the provision of funding will facilitate this. These firms are likely to go through several rounds of funding, each round diluting the equity stake of the founder. Once this falls below 50%, the founder will have effectively lost control of the business.

It is therefore very important that the strategic aims and objectives of the founder are aligned with the venture capitalist. Often this will be focused on a future 'exit', which can take the form of selling the business on to a larger firm, or going through an initial public offering (IPO), where the business becomes listed on a stock exchange and shares can be traded. It can be readily appreciated that it is better financially for an entrepreneur to own 20% of a £50 million business than 100% of a £5 million business.

Securing venture capital funding can be very difficult. Venture capitalists receive hundreds of business plans per year to consider and only invest in a relatively small number of these after a protracted due diligence process. This will also involve pitching the business, and the venture capitalist will make their decision based on their confidence in the entrepreneur as well as the business plan.

For example, does the entrepreneur have experience starting and growing a business, have they previously failed (and what did they learn), are they open and honest or are they secretive and evasive? All these factors will be taken into account before a decision is taken. The good news is that if a venture capitalist rejects your proposal there are many others to approach who may be more receptive. As with most aspects of entrepreneurship the key is not to give up!

7 Crowdfunding

A relatively recent development in start-up finance has been the emergence of crowdfunding, enabled by the internet and social media. Crowdfunding relies on raising finance through a high number of investors all making a small investment in return for either an equity stake or interest on the loan (sometimes called peer-to-peer lending). Often the investors will have a particular affinity for the new venture, and although they receive an equity stake the main motivation is to be able to support the venture. Crowdfunding is facilitated by firms such as Kickstarter and Seedrs, who manage the process on behalf of the entrepreneur and investors.

Management of resources, risk and radical innovation to drive high-growth firms

Whatever source of funding is selected for a new venture start-up it is highly likely that resource constraints will be a fact of life, particularly in the early years. In addition, decisions need to be taken regarding the level of risk that the entrepreneur is willing to undertake and the level of reward they hope to gain from the new venture.

Causation, effectuation and bricolage

A traditional perspective on entrepreneurship theory proposes that entrepreneurs identify and evaluate opportunities and then select a course of action that is the most appropriate to exploit the most promising opportunity.

This approach to entrepreneurial decision-making is sometimes referred to as 'causation', where the entrepreneur sets out to achieve a predetermined goal logically through rigorous planning and development of their business.

An alternative perspective views the entrepreneurial environment as much more uncertain, dynamic and interactive, with the entrepreneur relying more on their ability to react to changes and emergence rather than logical planning. This approach is referred to as 'effectuation', where rather than focusing on achieving predetermined goals the entrepreneur focuses on managing the factors they can directly control and responding to shifts in the environment with agility and savvy.

Regardless of whether entrepreneurs adopt causation or effectuation approaches the reality for start-ups is that they are likely to encounter resource constraints that limit their ability to deliver growth. These resources could be funding, infrastructure, labour or specialist skills and capabilities. Constraints in these areas can place start-ups at a competitive disadvantage to larger, more established firms.

Responses to these constraints could be to accept the reality of the situation and lower expectations and goals for the business. Alternatively the entrepreneur could focus their efforts on bridging the shortfall and securing the additional resources required. However, a body of research (e.g. Baker and Nelson, 2005) has highlighted a third approach to overcoming resource constraints, termed 'bricolage'.

Bricolage refers to making best use of the resources at hand, often recombining them in innovative ways that in themselves can provide new opportunities to the firm. The phrase 'necessity is the mother of invention' sums up this approach and plays to the natural problem-solving, creative and innovative capabilities of entrepreneurs. By adopting a bricolage approach start-ups can close the competitive gap between themselves and more established firms and potentially develop new opportunities for innovation.

Risk and radical innovation

Most innovations are low risk in nature. These 'incremental innovations' provide a series of small improvements in existing products, technologies, processes and services. Customers usually respond well to incremental innovation, and the investment required is relatively small. However, incremental innovations tend to be easy to copy and therefore yield no long-term competitive advantage. Greater payoffs can be achieved by investing in 'radical innovations', which deliver much higher levels of improvement, are much more difficult for competitors to copy and can potentially deliver a sustained market-leading position.

Firms that adopt a radical innovation approach can therefore offer superior and differentiated products and services compared with established firms that are locked into incremental innovation. The downside is that radical innovations are associated with inherently higher levels of risk and can be difficult bring to market. The exact delineation between incremental and radical innovation will vary between firms, markets and industry sectors and may in many cases be blurred and imprecise.

However, categorising innovations as incremental or radical using a risk versus reward trade-off is an important discipline. Research in this area (e.g. McDermott and O'Connor, 2002) suggests there are three broad strategic areas firms must consider when managing radical innovation projects: choice of market scope, competency development and the role of leaders, teams and networks.

1 Choice of market scope

When developing radical innovation programmes firms should start by considering the market scope. This will focus on either expanding an existing market or on creating a new market. When expanding an existing market firms need to focus on ensuring that the radical innovation programme delivers a substantial benefit over existing market offerings and that the threat of cannibalising existing product lines is fully considered. In addition, firms need to consider the level of market resistance to new technology and identify a strategy to overcome this.

When creating new markets firms need to focus on managing higher levels of inherent risk and uncertainty when compared to expanding an existing market and ensuring an effective business model is developed to fully take advantage of the potential offered by a market creating innovation. Firms also need to develop a strategy to convince a sufficient number of customers to enter the new market.

2 Competency development

Firms build up competencies over time that enable them to coordinate diverse production skills and integrate multiple streams of technology. However, for radical innovation programmes existing competencies need to be developed and expanded, presenting a significant organisational challenge.

Risk can be reduced by developing new competencies that are adjacent to the firm's existing competencies. For example, an aerospace firm with strong competencies in materials science could expand from steel to nickel and then into titanium products. This is a lower-risk route than having to develop brand new competencies in nonadjacent areas, such as aerodynamic modelling or fluid dynamics.

Developing alliances with external partners who already possess either technological or market competencies can also reduce the risk, time and investment required to develop these internally. Partners need to be carefully selected, and considerable attention must be given to the contractual framework governing areas such as intellectual property and the division of profits.

3 The role of leaders, teams and networks

Ultimately the success of a radical innovation programme with be determined by the individuals within the firm. Three key issues emerge with respect to the role of individuals: leadership, teams and networks.

There are two leadership roles that relate to radical innovation development. The first is the identification of 'senior sponsors' who are required to provide the financial backing and support for the programme and, if required, to defend it from premature termination. The second is to identify 'champions' who are required to provide the operational-level enthusiasm and energy to overcome hurdles and keep the programme moving forward towards achieving its goals. For a start-up the founding entrepreneur will be both sponsor and champion.

The importance of teams was introduced in Chapter 2. For radical innovation programmes teams require diversity in both breadth and depth of experience, including technical and marketing experience. Where the programme is a marked departure from the firm's current offerings then recruiting team members from outside the firm can strengthen the team.

Experienced team members will have specific roles and functions. However, they will also have developed deep informal networks within and outside the firm. These can provide access to information and knowledge that can be used to overcome problems and keep the programme on track.

New venture creation via corporate venturing

Innovation drives growth through the development of new products, services, processes and business models. However, for large and complex organisations the internal barriers to innovation are many. It often seems that somewhere along the line the entrepreneurial spirit that originally made the business successful has been lost. In an effort to overcome these barriers many established businesses turn to corporate venturing to launch new ventures, reignite entrepreneurship and kick-start growth.

34 *New venture start-up and growth*

Types of corporate venturing

Corporate venturing is nothing new. For example, in the 1960s and 1970s around 25% of the Fortune 500 companies ran corporate-venturing programmes. Well-known companies that have introduced corporate-venturing programmes include Adobe, Intel, Lucent, Exxon, Nokia, Cable & Wireless, Unilever, Procter & Gamble, British Telecom, Siemens, 3M and Xerox. Universities also spin-off ventures based on their scientific research and intellectual property. Corporate venturing generally takes one of three forms:

1 Internal corporate venturing (ICV)

Internal corporate venturing is when the company creates a new business that operates from within the company's organisational domain, often with a high degree of alignment with existing capabilities.

2 External corporate venturing (ECV)

External corporate venturing is when a company creates a new business that operates outside the company's organisational domain, so-called spin-offs or spin-outs. The parent will either wholly own or retain a significant equity stake in the new business.

3 Corporate venture capital (CVC)

Corporate venture capital is when a company invests in a start-up or early-phase company that has originated from outside the organisation. It therefore acts in a similar manner to a venture capitalist but with the potential benefits of a longer time horizon, larger funding available, and the support of the parent company's resources and capabilities.

Strategic impact of venturing

While companies will want to see a healthy financial return on their investment, corporate venturing often has a strong strategic element. For example, corporate venturing can:

- Infuse the company with an entrepreneurial dynamic that promotes further innovation and growth across the core business.
- Enable the company to experiment with and pilot disruptive technologies that may support the core business, become the future core of the business or provide opportunities to move into adjacent markets.

- Develop complementary businesses that create demand for the company's core products and services. For example, Intel invested in businesses that drove demand for its microprocessors.
- Enable the company to attract, motivate and retain talented employees. This is particularly important for technical specialists who may be tempted to leave and form their own venture capital–backed start-up.
- Provide commercialisation opportunities for technologies developed by R&D that do not fit the company's core business, thereby increasing the return on R&D investment.
- Drive overall company strategy; or in some cases corporate venturing actually is the company strategy (e.g. Richard Branson's Virgin Group).

Turning the archetypal slow, lumbering and bureaucratic corporate 'elephant' into a fast, nimble, and entrepreneurial business-creating machine is quite difficult to achieve, as witnessed by the extensive list of failed venturing programmes.

For example, Lucent Technologies' New Ventures Group was set up to commercialise technology developed from the Bell Laboratory. However, following the telecom downturn Lucent sold 80% of its interests in the New Ventures Group to the British private capital management company Coller Capital in 2002.

So, what can be done to improve the chances of successful corporate venturing? Research (e.g. Covin and Miles, 2007) points to several common themes:

1 Build leadership capability

Leaders should view corporate venturing as an integrated and continuous component of the strategy-making process. This means all senior executives should share a commitment for corporate venturing.

2 Establish realistic expectations

Corporate venturing is a long-term commitment, not a short-term exercise to shore-up the company's finances. Corporate ventures therefore need to be protected from unrealistic expectations. Similarly, measuring the performance of corporate ventures with the same metrics used for measuring the established core business should be avoided.

3 Manage with a portfolio mindset

Companies should focus on developing a portfolio of corporate-venturing projects that spread risk and allow for the failure or cancellation of individual projects. It is the performance of the overall portfolio that should be the primary concern of senior management.

4 Capture knowledge and learning

Successful corporate-venturing programmes deliver more than simply financial returns. The knowledge and learning generated from corporate ventures are key outputs and must be captured and incorporated into the core business.

Overall corporate venturing can make an important contribution to a company's financial position, strategy development and knowledge base. Corporate venturing provides an effective mechanism to escape the constraints of the core business and explore new opportunities that will sustain innovation, entrepreneurism and growth.

Innovation and entrepreneurship in action: Primordial Radio

Primordial Radio is a rock and metal internet radio service launched in 2017 with the firm intention of doing things differently. Founders Hugh Evans, Russ Collington, Pete Bailey and Ben Woodhouse had met while working for Team Rock Radio, a venture capital–backed enterprise which failed, with losses of over £20 million. In the aftermath the four friends decided there had to be a better way to run a radio service that would focus on the needs of listeners in addition to being financially sustainable. So, rather than seek new employment they decided to challenge the status quo and launch their new venture. Reflecting on the decision to become entrepreneurs, CEO Hugh Evans recalls, *"we felt we had a good idea, but why should someone else do it, why not us, what have we got to lose?"*

The traditional model for commercial radio is essentially based on offering a free service, attracting a large audience and then generating income through advertising revenue—the larger the audience the higher the advertising rates. However, there are disadvantages to this model. Firstly, overheads tend to be high. For example, an annual DAB broadcasting licence can cost well over £100,000, and expensive studios are also required. Secondly, AM/FM and DAB broadcasters are regulated by Ofcom and can be fined if deemed to be in breach of standards.

But according to Evans, perhaps the biggest flaw is that ultimately commercial radio stations are run for the benefit of advertisers, not listeners. This means the music played tends to stick to a narrow selection of artists and 'classic' songs, limiting choice and also not supporting the new upcoming bands that are the future of the scene. Adverts fill 20% of airtime, further limiting the music that can be played and diminishing the listener experience. As argued by Evans, "*commercial radio stations aren't really free, because they steal your time by making you listen to adverts.*"

The Primordial Radio approach turns this model on its head. Firstly, rather than broadcasting through DAB or AM/FM Primordial Radio has utilised the internet, taking advantage of recent advances in broadband, Wi-Fi, and 5G technology and benefiting from the growing adoption of smartphones to access internet content. This has also meant that broadcasting licences are not required because there is no Ofcom regulation, and DJs can broadcast from home rather than a studio, further reducing overheads.

Secondly, Primordial Radio is a paid subscription service with no advertising. Listeners have access to a free stream and a three-month trial period and then pay a monthly or annual membership subscription to access the service. By generating revenues from subscriptions instead of advertising, Primordial Radio is free to offer a much wider range of music that reflects the preferences of their members, including supporting new bands. Thirdly, revenues are further developed through selling branded merchandise, such as clothing, and by hosting ticketed membership events and music gigs.

The Primordial Radio model is a radical departure for the commercial broadcasting sector, and most industry experts believed it could not work. Who would pay to listen to music that could be accessed for free by rival stations? Undeterred, the founders pressed ahead and considered the options for financing their new venture. Seeking venture capital funding was rejected early on due to the experience of the demise of Team Rock Radio and the feeling that the business would lose its independence. Applying for a bank loan was also rejected because the unproven nature of the radical business model would mean banks would either reject the application as too risky or apply a very high interest rate and strict lending conditions.

This led the founders to consider a third option, crowdfunding. Using social media such as Facebook, Twitter and Instagram Primordial Radio reached out to the rock and metal community to directly ask for investment via the equity crowdfunding platform Seedrs. Over 800 investors responded, raising over £130,000 and valuing the fledgling business at £850,000. The investors also made up the station's initial core listeners, strengthening the bond between Primordial Radio and its members. In addition, members and investors have also provided a range of help and professional support, expanding the resources available to establish and develop the business.

The directors of Primordial Radio have ambitious plans for the future. The membership base has expanded to over 1,500 paying members, and there are now 12 DJs. A wide range of events and music gigs have been organised, and even the Annual General Meeting serves as a two-day event which includes camping, bands, and the opportunity to sample their very own beer, 'Primordial Süp'. A second round of crowdfunding raised a further £140,000, and the business valuation increased to £1.1 million.

But arguably it has been the building of a likeminded and socially responsible community of music fans from across the UK and wider that has been Primordial Radio's greatest success, underpinned by six 'pillars' of music, community, innovation, fun, mental health and environment. According to Evans the aim is to grow the business to a position where 70% of profits are reinvested in the business, 20% returned as dividends to investors and 10% donated to charitable causes, such as Manchester Mind and The Sophie Lancaster Foundation.

Ultimately the founders of Primordial Radio have created an innovative and unique rock and metal service owned and shaped by the community it serves. Could they ever go back to being employees? According to Evans, the answer is a firm no!

Discussion and reflection activity

1. How likely are you to start your own new venture within the next five years? What factors make this an attractive option? What factors are barriers? How might they be overcome?
2. If you were to start your own new venture what type of funding would you choose, and why?
3. What resource constraints does your organisation face, and could a bricolage approach help mitigate these?
4. How would you characterise your organisation in relation to its tolerance for risk and appetite for radical innovation?
5. What are the opportunities for corporate venturing within your organisation? How would corporate venturing be beneficial to your organisation?
6. What opportunities and constraints does Primordial Radio face? How would you advise the directors of Primordial Radio to develop the next phase of growth?

Recommended reading

Baker, T. and Nelson, R. E. (2005). Creating Something From Nothing: Resource Construction Through Entrepreneurial Bricolage. *Administrative Science Quarterly*, 50(3), 329–366.

Behrens, J. and Patzelt, H. (2018). Incentives, Resources and Combinations of Innovation Radicalness and Innovation Speed. *British Journal of Management*, 29, 691–711.

Burgelman, R. A. and Välikangas, L. (2005). Managing Internal Corporate Venturing Cycles. *MIT Sloan Management Review*, 46(4), 26–34.

Chesbrough, H. (2002). Making Sense of Corporate Venture Capital. *Harvard Business Review*, 80(3), 90–99.

Covin, J. G. and Miles, M. P. (2007). Strategic Use of Corporate Venturing. *Entrepreneurship Theory and Practice*, 31(2), 183–207.

Drover, W., Busenitz, L., Matusik, S., Townsend, D., Anglin, A. and Dushnitsky, G. (2017). A Review and Road Map of Entrepreneurial Equity Financing Research: Venture Capital, Corporate Venture Capital, Angel Investment, Crowdfunding, and Accelerators. *Journal of Management*, 43(6), 1820–1853.

Dyer, J. H., Gregersen, H. B. and Christensen, C. (2008). Entrepreneur Behaviours, Opportunity Recognition and the Origins of Innovative Ventures. *Strategic Entrepreneurship Journal*, 2(4), 317–338.

Enkel, E. and Sagmeister, V. (2020). External Corporate Venturing Modes as a New Way to Develop Dynamic Capabilities. *Technovation*, 96. https://doi.org/10.1016/j.technovation.2020.102128.

Fisher, G. (2012). Effectuation, Causation, and Bricolage: A Behavioural Comparison of Emerging Theories in Entrepreneurship Research. *Entrepreneurship Theory and Practice*, 36(5), 1019–1051.

Kloyz, F. (2016). How to Succeed with Radical Innovation. *MIT Sloan Management Review*, 58(1), 107–112.

Lovallo, D., Koller, T., Uhlaner, R. and Kahneman, D. (2020). Your Company is Too Risk-Averse: Here's Why and What To Do About It. *Harvard Business Review*, 98(2), 104–111.

McDermott, C. and O'Connor, G. (2002). Managing Radical Innovation: An Overview of Emergent Strategy Issues. *Journal of Product Innovation Management*, 19(1), 424–438.

McGrath, R., Keil, T. and Tukiainen, T. (2006). Extracting Value from Corporate Venturing. *MIT Sloan Management Review*, 48(1), 50–56.

Sarasvathy, S. (2001). Causation and Effectuation: Toward a Theoretical Shift from Inevitability to Entrepreneurial Contingency. *Academy of Management Review*, 26(2), 243–265.

Weiblen, T. and Chesbrough, H. W. (2015). Engaging with Start-Ups to Enhance Corporate Innovation. *California Management Review*, 57, 66–90.

4 Developing and sustaining innovative and entrepreneurial organisations

Essential summary

1 The role of leader is crucial to develop and sustain innovative and entrepreneurial organisations. Steve Jobs, the co-founder and CEO of Apple, is often used as an exemplar of leadership for innovation. Although Jobs is often characterised as having an abrasive management style five broad leadership insights into developing and sustaining innovation and entrepreneurship emerge:

   - Focus.
   - Simplicity.
   - Intuition.
   - Reinvention.
   - High-performance environment.

2 Organisational Ambidexterity is the ability of a firm to exploit the core business while still devoting sufficient resources to explore opportunities for new products, services and markets. Finding a balance between exploitation and exploration is difficult because the day-to-day needs of running the core business tend to take priority and consume both resources and executive time and attention. To foster ambidexterity managers can focus on two areas:

   - **Structural Ambidexterity:** How the internal and external configuration of the organisation can be optimised to develop ambidexterity.
   - **Contextual Ambidexterity:** The role of the individual in the development of an ambidextrous organisation.

3 It has been argued that the really big opportunities from innovation come not from new products or services in themselves but by focusing attention on how to develop new ways of managing organisations, or

Developing and sustaining organisations 41

so-called Management Innovation. Examples of firms that have benefited from Management Innovation include General Electric, Procter & Gamble, General Motors and Toyota. Organisations looking for Management Innovation opportunities should explore:

- Current trade-offs, for example, cost versus quality.
- What they are currently bad at, for example, managing change.
- Emerging challenges, for example, rapidly changing technology and consumer preferences.

Leading innovative and entrepreneurial organisations

Apple is the Silicon Valley–based technology company responsible for launching the Apple Lisa PC, the Apple Newton Message Pad, the Apple Pippin Games Console, the Apple eMate 300 and the Power Mac G4 Cube. Amongst these commercial disappointments Apple also launched some fairly successful products, such as the MacBook, iMac, iPod, iPhone, and iPad, becoming the world's most valuable company in the process. The entrepreneurial and innovative leader credited with Apple's success is co-founder and CEO Steve Jobs.

The commercial success of Apple, its steady stream of market-defining products, and the untimely death of Jobs in October 2011 from pancreatic cancer, has led to a slew of books and articles analysing his impact on the business. In particular there has been a focus on identifying and distilling the lessons that can be learned from Jobs on leadership, innovation and entrepreneurship. The message seems to be clear: If you want your company to be as innovative as Apple, you must lead like Jobs. From this, five broad leadership insights into developing and sustaining innovation and entrepreneurship emerge:

1 Focus

When Jobs was asked to return to lead Apple in 1997 he found a vast portfolio of different computers and peripherals, including multiple versions of the Macintosh. New product development was eating through cash reserves, and customers were confused as to what to buy, so they ended up not buying anything. A company can only tolerate rising costs and falling revenues for so long, and Jobs took a ruthless approach. Apple was now to focus on developing just four "great" products serving well-defined market segments. All other products and development programmes were cancelled with immediate effect. The new strategy worked and set the platform for future success.

2 Simplicity

Surely innovative technology-based products should be complex and difficult to use without reading some sort of manual. For Apple the opposite philosophy was applied. Innovation meant simplifying both hardware and software to make the user experience as easy and intuitive as possible. Jobs hired Jonathan Ive to head the industrial design team with a clear mandate to simplify Apple products, even extending to product packaging and the design of unseen circuit boards. The result was a new generation of sleek, distinctive, desirable and premium products that came to define the Apple brand.

3 Intuition

Jobs believed strongly in his own innate ability to identify breakthrough products and new markets and bypassed the whole expensive business of conducting market research, in effect becoming a one-man focus group relying on intuition rather than mountains of marketing data and consumer insights. A famous quote attributed to Henry Ford is that if he had asked his customers what they wanted they would have said *"a faster horse."* Jobs took this approach to heart, believing that customers don't necessarily know what they want until they are actually shown breakthrough products. Jobs designed products that he wanted to use himself. For example, as a music fan he wanted a simple portable device that could carry a thousand songs, an idea that became the hugely successful iPod.

4 Reinvention

One of the great innovation myths is the belief that you need to come up with brand new, never-before-seen, and unique products that are inspired through a flash of creative genius. However, it can be equally powerful to follow a path of reinvention and repositioning of existing products. Apple was not the first company to launch personal computers, MP3 type music players, smartphones or tablets. However, when they did enter these markets they offered products that were significantly differentiated from existing products and positioned Apple as the leader. For example, the iPhone was positioned as a premium-priced device that was *"way smarter and way easier to use"* than any existing smartphone. When launching the iPhone at Macworld 2007 Jobs declared *"today, Apple reinvents the phone!"*

5 High-performance environment

Jobs is often characterised as a perfectionist. Words such as 'impatient', 'petulant', 'rough', 'stormy' and 'rude', have been used to describe his management style. Personally, I don't advocate this style of leadership, although the counter argument is that in the case of Apple it clearly got results.

Getting angry on a regular basis is not in itself a pathway to high performance. So, Jobs also ensured that he was surrounded by an exceptionally talented, hardworking and presumably very well-remunerated team with a passion to succeed. One of the driving factors behind the success of Silicon Valley is that the high density of technology firms generates a highly dynamic market for talent. Employees unhappy with Jobs's management style could easily move on to another company, yet it seemed as though Jobs had the ability to inspire a high degree of loyalty within Apple.

As well as a focus on talent and individual performance, Jobs was also a strong believer in facilitating informal meetings to promote idea sharing and creativity, as opposed to emails, memos and formal PowerPoint presentations. For example, as CEO at Pixar he redesigned the building to encourage unplanned collaborations. The main doors, stairs and corridors all led to the central atrium where the café and mailboxes were also located. This encouraged mingling and spontaneous meetings between people that otherwise might not come into contact.

Organisational Ambidexterity

The term 'Organisational Ambidexterity' was first used in 1976 by Professor Robert Duncan but gained traction following Professor James March's 1991 influential paper 'Exploration and exploitation in organizational learning'. Since then a body of research suggests that ambidextrous firms are more adept at managing the internal tension and conflicting demands between allocating resources to run the core business while dedicating sufficient resources to develop new products and services that can meet future customer requirements. Managing the current needs of the core business is said to require an 'exploitation' mindset. Focusing on developing future opportunities is said to require an 'exploration' mindset.

Early studies suggested that balancing these trade-offs within the organisation was unachievable, and firms should focus on only performing one of these at a time. However, more recent research (e.g. Birkinshaw, Hamel and Mol, 2008) proposes that not only can the balance be achieved, it is essential for success in the medium term and for survival in the longer term. Examples of the consequences of failing to achieve this balance include

Kodak, whose failure to adopt new digital technologies led to loss of market share to competitors like Fujitsu.

However, exploitation of the firm's resources to serve the existing market is still an important consideration. It is this which generates revenues and cash flow, allowing the firm to pay staff and creditors. Firms that fail to have a tight focus on cash flow, particularly small to medium enterprises (SMEs), tend to go out of business quickly. Larger publicly listed companies are required to meet short-term quarterly performance targets for their investors, who demand steady and consistent growth and are happy to fire chief executives who fail to deliver this. For these reasons most companies have a strong focus on exploitation via operational efficiency and execution, demanding a significant degree of resource and executive attention.

Exploration requires a very different approach involving search, experimentation and discovery. Exploration is more speculative and has less-predictable outcomes, requiring a higher tolerance for risk and ambiguity. It also does not deliver immediate returns, requiring investment over a sustained period of time before revenues and profits are generated. For these reasons it can be much more difficult to make the case for investment in exploration in the face of the pressing current needs of the business.

So, the question researchers have focused on is essentially a very practical one: What can firms actually do to achieve ambidexterity and balance the demands of both exploitation and exploration? From this line of enquiry two key areas have emerged: 'Structural Ambidexterity' and 'Contextual Ambidexterity'.

Structural Ambidexterity

Structural Ambidexterity examines how the internal and external configuration of the organisation can be optimised to develop ambidexterity. Traditional configurations such as the simple functional structure are efficient in allocating resources to support the current business, that is, exploitation. However, the inherent rigidity of the functional structure can limit exploration activities. The formation of cross-functional teams operating within the organisation but outside the existing management hierarchy can be an effective solution for delivering exploration within a functional structure.

A second option is to establish formal business units alongside existing functions specifically to manage exploration, for example, R&D and business development departments. This has the advantage of having clearly dedicated resources separate from the firm's day-to-day activities. However, there is a danger that these units can become isolated from the wider organisation, and therefore opportunities for new products and services developed in exploration-focused business units are not commercialised.

Developing and sustaining organisations 45

A third option is to establish project teams that are not only responsible for exploring new opportunities but are also responsible for bringing these to market. They mirror the structure of the existing business, with their own manufacturing, sales and marketing functions. In this way there is integration between the exploiting side of the business and the exploring side of the business, each with equal weighting and supporting a fully ambidextrous organisation.

A fourth option to consider is the role of organisations that are external to the business. For example, the establishment of joint ventures or strategic outsourcing may facilitate the development of ambidexterity. External relationships can provide a channel to escape the constraints of the internal structure, allowing access to new knowledge, talent, thinking and market opportunities.

Contextual Ambidexterity

Contextual Ambidexterity considers the role of the individual in the development of an ambidextrous organisation. In this context individuals range from senior executives to front-line workers, linked by a shared set of behaviours and attributes which together help foster ambidexterity, including:

- Being action-orientated, taking the initiative and being alert to opportunities beyond the boundaries of their own roles.
- Being networkers, brokers and cooperative team players who seek opportunities to combine their efforts with others.
- Being highly motivated with a tolerance for risk and ambiguity and often acting without seeking permission or support from superiors.

Although staff operate with a high degree of independence and autonomy the role of the senior management team in developing an ambidextrous organisation is still key. Senior management set the strategic direction of the company, define the organisational structure and decide what the balance between exploitation and exploration should be. They also develop and define key processes and policies, such as recruitment, reward and staff development. Senior management must communicate a compelling company vision to stakeholders and resolve internal conflicts and disputes over resource allocation.

Managers tasked with developing an ambidextrous organisation need to consider both Structural and Contextual Ambidexterity as complementary factors which must both be addressed. The right structure with the wrong behaviours is likely to be ineffective. Similarly, even individuals with the right behaviours can be rendered ineffective without the right structure.

46 *Developing and sustaining organisations*

What is clear is that while Organisational Ambidexterity is difficult to achieve it can deliver enhanced long-term performance for organisations that can find the right balance between exploitation and exploration.

Management Innovation

Up to this point we have generally framed innovation outputs in terms of either new 'products' (e.g. an iPhone) or new 'services' (e.g. iTunes). However, some researchers argue that the focus should be on how to develop new ways of managing organisations, or 'Management Innovation'. Perhaps the most vocal champion of Management Innovation is Professor Gary Hamel, who provides the following definition:

> *Management Innovation is a marked departure from traditional management principles, processes, and practices or a departure from customary organisational forms that significantly alters the way the work of management is performed.*

Examples of Management Innovation

Hamel (2006) cites several examples of organisations that have reaped the rewards of introducing radically different management techniques, including:

General Electric

General Electric (GE) developed the first industrial-scale R&D capability in the early 1900s. This innovation brought management discipline to the process of scientific discovery, leading to the granting of more patents than any other US company over the next 50 years. GE has extended this approach to systematically developing exceptional leaders, for example, by training at its purpose-built Crotonville educational facility, implementing 360-degree feedback and rigorously measuring management performance.

Procter & Gamble

Procter & Gamble (P&G) developed the first formalised approach to brand management in the 1930s. This allowed the company to steadily develop a diverse product portfolio with enhanced value through the intangible asset of brands such as Tide detergent, Crest toothpaste, Gillette razors, and Olay skin care. Today, P&G is one of the first major adopters of the 'Open Innovation' model of developing external links to provide access to new technologies and market opportunities (see Chapter 6).

General Motors

General Motors is credited with developing the divisional organisational structure in response to the problem of how to effectively manage the vast family of companies and products that had evolved since its formation. The new structure, designed by Alfred P. Sloan in the 1930s, established a centralised executive committee that set policy and exercised financial control alongside operating divisions organised by product and responsible for day-to-day operations.

Toyota

Toyota has been able to take a significant market share from US rivals by producing low-cost, high-quality and reliable cars. But behind this formula is their capability to drive continuous improvement by giving production-line employees the skills, tools and permission to solve problems as they arise and to head off new problems before they occur. This system is in marked contrast to the US system of expecting employees to be cogs in an automated production line.

Opportunities for Management Innovation

According to Hamel, the foundation of Management Innovation is to purposely and systematically focus on identifying and solving a big management problem. The bigger the problem, the bigger the opportunity to generate a breakthrough that leads to a significant competitive advantage. To do this organisations should ask three simple but searching questions:

1 What are your current trade-offs?

Business and management are full of trade-offs, such as quality versus cost, standardisation versus customisation, make versus buy, consolidation versus expansion, simplicity versus complexity and focus versus diversification. Management Innovation is often driven by the desire to break these types of trade-offs. For example, open-source software development requires the combination of two seemingly incompatible ideas: radical decentralisation with disciplined large-scale project management. And as previously highlighted, Toyota produced high quality at low cost through the innovation of continuous improvement.

2 What is your organisation bad at?

If you are being honest, this should produce a pretty long list. This can include resistance to change, inability to spot market shifts, poor implementation of

48 *Developing and sustaining organisations*

improvement projects and failure to fully tap into the energy and creativity of employees. However, these problems are your opportunity to develop radical solutions through Management Innovation.

3 What are your emerging challenges?

If you thought addressing your current organisational deficiencies was tough, try looking into the future at your emerging challenges: ever-accelerating technological change, rapidly increasing customer power, low-cost competitors and new market entrants, even social and political resistance regarding 'big business'. These challenges will demand that organisations develop Management Innovation capabilities to remain competitive.

Developing Management Innovation

What can managers do to develop their organisation's capacity for Management Innovation? Research (e.g. Birkinshaw and Mol, 2006) suggests there are four key areas:

1 Create a questioning and problem-solving culture

Developing Management Innovation relies on engaging all of the organisation's employees to focus on overcoming unusual management problems or challenges. It's not just a top-down directive. If you don't already have a questioning and problem-solving culture, then congratulations, developing one is your first Management Innovation challenge!

2 Identify analogies and exemplars from different environments

Exposing employees to different types of environments can help provide the insights required to solve management problems. For example, if a commercial organisation wants to improve employee motivation and engagement, studying the not-for-profit sector, open-source software development, or sports teams can provide analogies and exemplars that enable innovative solutions to be developed.

3 Build a capacity for low-risk experimentation

It would be a mistake to attempt a full-scale launch of multiple Management Innovation programmes across an organisation. This may lead to confusion and even organisational paralysis. Instead, organisations should aim to develop an experimental model where ideas can be tested on a small scale for a limited period of time before evaluation. Only once an idea has been shown to deliver business benefits should it be rolled out. For an experimental model to work the funding for small-scale trials needs to be made available, as well securing senior management project sponsorship.

4 Use external change agents to explore new ideas

There is value in selectively making use of academics and consultants in developing Management Innovation. External agents can represent a source of new ideas from different environments, act as a sounding board for Management Innovation development and help evaluate and validate Management Innovation programme outcomes.

Innovation and entrepreneurship in action: 3M

Developing and sustaining innovative and entrepreneurial organisations is challenging. One organisation which has often been held up as an exemplar is the US industrial conglomerate 3M. Founded in 1902 as the Minnesota Mining and Manufacturing Company, 3M is now a billion-dollar turnover Fortune 500 company which produces a staggering 60,000 products in areas such as abrasives, adhesives, personal protective equipment, laminates, insulation, medical products and electrical circuits. Maintaining innovation within such a complex organisation is of vital importance to develop multiple new product lines for diverse market sectors. To achieve this 3M have placed innovation at the heart of their organisation and pioneered new ways to manage innovation and engage employees.

3M's leadership have set a clear objective for the company: To become the most innovative company in the world. This is an audacious goal but succeeds in aligning all areas of the business to a common cause. To support this 3M requires each of its businesses to deliver at least 30% of sales from products that did not exist four years ago. Top managers at 3M see one of their major duties as facilitating innovation. Promotions are often from within, meaning people build up an in-depth understanding of the business and a strong network. Redundancy programmes are avoided, as are short-term contracts as these can damage loyalty and commitment to share knowledge and innovate.

New employees quickly adsorb the company's stories and traditions. These reinforce the values and atmosphere that encourage information sharing and innovation. Somewhat counter-intuitively 3M stories often centre on employees who disregard management and continue to develop products that they believe in, for example, Dick Drew's development of Scotch Tape in the 1920s. The company has a relatively high tolerance for mistakes to encourage staff to experiment, make decisions and take some risks.

3M looks for people who want to start new things, rather than run the existing business. They are action orientated, self-motivated, have a multidisciplinary approach and are keen to network and learn new skills. Retaining such people requires developing an environment in which they can flourish, for example, by the provision of time, funding and recognition. 3M initiated a '15% rule', which means that staff can spend 15% of their time working on innovative projects of their own choosing. As well as time, 3M provides small grants to develop new technical ideas, for example, buying specialist equipment. The company also has a dual promotion system, where non-management specialists can progress to Vice-President level based on their technical contribution. There are also several award programmes in recognition of innovation.

It's worth remembering that this is not a rigid prescription for success. What works at 3M may not be appropriate for other organisations. However, policies such as the 15% rule have been successfully adopted by Google to drive innovation and attract talented employees. Overall the strong focus on innovation and the integration of strategic goals with innovation-supporting policies has paid dividends for 3M.

Discussion and reflection activity

1. What could you do as a leader to help develop and sustain innovation and entrepreneurship within your organisation?
2. What do you feel are the main factors which have led to the success of Apple?
3. Has your organisation got the right balance between exploitation and exploration? If not, what steps could be taken to address this?
4. What are your organisation's current trade-offs and emergent challenges? What is your organisation currently bad at?
5. What are the opportunities for Management Innovation within your organisation?
6. What aspects of 3M's approach for developing and sustaining innovation could be adopted by your organisation?

Recommended reading

Birkinshaw, J., Hamel, G. and Mol, M. (2008). Management Innovation. *Academy of Management Review*, 33(4), 825–845.

Birkinshaw, J. and Mol, M. (2006). How Management Innovation Happens. *MIT Sloan Management Review*, 47(4), 81–88.

Boh, W. F., Evaristo, R. and Ouderkirk, A. (2014). Balancing Breadth and Depth of Expertise for Innovation: A 3M Story. *Research Policy*, 43(2), 349–366.

Brand, A. (1998). Knowledge Management and Innovation at 3M. *Journal of Knowledge Management*, 2(1), 17–22.

Garud, R., Gehman, J. and Kumaraswamy, A. (2011). Complexity Arrangements for Sustained Innovation: Lessons from 3M Corporation. *Organization Studies*, 32(6), 737–767.

Hamel, G. (2006). The Why, What, and How of Management Innovation. *Harvard Business Review*, 84(2), 72–84.

Hughs, D. J., Lee, A., Tian, A.W., Newman, A. and Legood, A. (2018). Leadership, Creativity, and Innovation: A Critical Review and Practical Recommendations. *Leadership Quarterly*, 29(5), 549–569.

Isaacson, W. (2012). The Real Leadership Lessons of Steve Jobs. *Harvard Business Review*, 90(4), 92–102.

Khosravi, P., Newton, C. and Rezvani, A. (2019). Management Innovation: A Systematic Review and Meta-Analysis of Past Decades of Research. *European Management Journal*, 37(6), 694–707.

March, J. G. (1991). Exploration and Exploitation in Organizational Learning. *Organization Science*, 2, 71–87.

O'Reilly III, C. H. and Tushman, M. L. (2011). Organisational Ambidexterity in Action: How Managers Explore and Exploit. *California Management Review*, 53(4), 5–22.

Podolny, J. and Hansen, M. (2020). How Apple is Organized for Innovation. *Harvard Business Review*, 98(6), 86–95.

Renko, M., Tarabishy, A. E., Carsrud, A. L. and Brannback, M. (2015). Understanding and Measuring Entrepreneurial Leadership Style. *Journal of Small Business Management*, 53, 54–74.

Rosing, K., Frese, M. and Bausch, A. (2011). Explaining the Heterogeneity of the Leadership-Innovation Relationship: Ambidextrous Leadership. *Leadership Quarterly*, 22(5), 956–974.

von Hippel, E., Thomke, S. and Sonnack, M. (1999). Creating Breakthroughs at 3M. *Harvard Business Review*, 77, 47–57.

5 Knowledge Management, collaboration and User-Centred Innovation

Essential summary

1   Knowledge Management can be thought of as:

    The organisational system that acquires, stores and provides access to information, experience and expertise in order to create new capabilities, support innovation, and drive performance.

    Knowledge Management is distinct from innovation but has a major role in developing the capability to innovate. There are two broad approaches that organisations can utilise to manage knowledge: codification and personalisation.

    - **Codification:** Knowledge is carefully collated and stored on databases, where it can be accessed and used by anyone within the company as required.
    - **Personalisation:** Knowledge is closely tied to the person who developed it and is shared mainly through interpersonal contact.

2   The term 'Triple Helix' was established by Stanford Professor Henry Etzkowitz to help conceptualise the interaction between universities, industry and government that drives innovation, entrepreneurship and economic development. At the heart of the Triple Helix paradigm is the emergence of the so-called Entrepreneurial University, where economic development has become a core mission. The Entrepreneurial University has therefore moved from a generator of new knowledge to both a generator and commercialiser of new knowledge.

3   User-Centred Innovation is a model developed by MIT Professor Eric von Hippel, where users are able to innovate for themselves and are no longer reliant on firms pursuing traditional Manufacturing-Centred Innovation. The advantage of User-Centred Innovation is that users get

exactly what they want by utilising their knowledge of how a product or service works in practice to customise and optimise performance. Key to the User-Centred Innovation model is the identification and engagement of 'Lead Users' who are at the leading edge of the market and are significantly ahead of most other users. Firms that identify and collaborate with Lead Users can develop and enhance their opportunities for innovation.

Knowledge Management

The Austrian economist and management expert Peter Drucker foresaw the development of what he termed the 'knowledge economy'. In the knowledge economy growth is dependent on the quantity, quality and accessibility of the information available to 'knowledge workers', rather than the physical means of production, such as factories.

This shift in thinking initiated the trend for the outsourcing of production from Western economies to low-cost emerging economies, such as China. Western governments have responded by increasing the supply of knowledge workers, for example, by raising the number of graduates. The area of Knowledge Management has therefore become increasingly important, particularly in respect to how knowledge drives innovation and competitive advantage.

There are many definitions of Knowledge Management, and for the purposes of this book I offer the following:

> *Knowledge Management is the organisational system that acquires, stores and provides access to information, experience and expertise to create new capabilities, support innovation and drive performance.*

Knowledge Management, innovation and strategy

The previous definition shows that while Knowledge Management is distinct from innovation it has a major role in developing the capability to innovate. In this context Knowledge Management:

- Provides a focus in the organisation for the value of knowledge, creating an environment for the creation, sharing and leveraging of knowledge.
- Provides the mechanisms for knowledge to be stored and easily retrieved, growing the organisation's overall knowledge base.
- Can be used to convert tacit knowledge (i.e. the knowledge acquired by individuals over time) into explicit knowledge (i.e. knowledge that can be written down, retrieved and utilised by any individual).

- Facilitates collaboration across internal organisational boundaries, for example, via online forums and cross-functional knowledge-focused projects.
- Encourages collaboration with external partners who can provide or contribute to the development of new knowledge.
- Contributes to the development of the competencies and skills required for the innovation process by exposing staff to a wider knowledge base.
- Assists in the identification of gaps in the knowledge base and provides processes to fill those gaps to support innovation.
- Can facilitate the development of a knowledge-driven organisational culture within which innovation can be encouraged.

The strategic decision on whether to generate new knowledge internally (e.g. from in-house R&D) or to utilise external sources of knowledge (e.g. strategic alliances or licencing) is a key consideration. Research (e.g. Tidd and Trewhella, 1997) has suggested that there are two broad sets of issues that influence this decision. The first set is concerned with the organisation itself, for example, the corporate strategy, technological competencies, company culture towards external sources of knowledge and familiarity with the technology under consideration. These organisational aspects are termed 'inheritance factors'.

The second set is concerned with the characteristics and potential utility of the technology under consideration. These 'technological factors' can include the competitive impact of the technology, complexity, potential market impact, customer perception and the costs and timescales associated with developing internally. The consideration of both inheritance factors and technological factors will strongly influence the decision on whether to acquire new knowledge and technology internally or to seek external sources.

Codification and personalisation

Implementing a Knowledge Management strategy is often a difficult and daunting undertaking. Just how do you capture the knowledge of, for example, a hundred-year-old company with 100,000 employees operating in several distinct global markets? One of the big mistakes is to see Knowledge Management as just another IT project. While IT can help facilitate Knowledge Management, this in itself is unlikely to be successful without anchoring Knowledge Management to the overall strategy and developing an organisational culture aligned with Knowledge Management values. Knowledge Management strategies broadly fall into two approaches: codification and personalisation.

A codification strategy requires knowledge to be carefully collated and stored on databases, where it can be accessed and used by anyone within the company as required. This requires a high dependence on IT systems, such as document readers, and the discipline to input the knowledge generated by each and every consulting engagement. This allows the organisation to utilise a knowledge asset many times, with associated economies of scale (once the initial investment in IT is made).

For a personalisation strategy knowledge is closely tied to the person who developed it and is shared mainly through interpersonal contact. The primary role of IT systems is to facilitate the sharing of this information, not the storing of it. This allows the organisation to provide creative, analytically rigorous advice on high-level strategic problems by channelling individual expertise.

Which approach is best? It can be very difficult to codify tacit knowledge and retain the subtle detail and nuances found in face-to-face communication. For example, Xerox attempted to capture all the knowledge of their service and repair technicians in a database. However, this system reduced the time the technicians spent together sharing stories and tips on how they had fixed problems with the machines, reducing their overall effectiveness.

However, personalisation also has limitations. If the individual is the primary actor as both knowledge creator and the repository of knowledge, then what is to stop the source of your competitive advantage from simply walking out the door? To avoid this firms must focus on developing an organisational culture and a reward and recognition system that engages and motivates employees and supports both Knowledge Management and innovation.

University, government and industry collaboration: the Triple Helix model

Professor Henry Etzkowitz coined the term 'Triple Helix' in the 1990s to illustrate the interaction between universities, industry and government that drives innovation, entrepreneurship and economic development. Governments like economic development, particularly if it can be shown that their policies are contributing to it. There has therefore been no shortage of research funding to explore the Triple Helix paradigm to inform policy decisions aimed at forging closer links between universities and industry.

Universities are keen to research their own contribution to innovation driven economic development, particularly if it attracts a large amount of research funding. There has therefore been a significant focus on developing the understanding of the Triple Helix in recent years, especially in the European Union and United States, with the emergence of books, journal publications, specialist conferences and the founding of the Triple Helix Association.

Industry is increasingly interested in using universities to complement, and in some cases substitute, the expensive business of conducting in-house R&D. In particular, using universities to conduct early-stage speculative 'blue sky' research is highly cost effective, especially if this research is supported by government research grants and performed by knowledgeable and hardworking academics in well-equipped facilities. Overall, industry is looking to gain access to new technology and knowledge to deliver a competitive advantage in the market, and this contributes to the overall economic development that governments seek to promote.

According to Etzkowitz there are four dimensions that contribute to the development of the Triple Helix:

1   The separate change and development of each of the three helices, for example, through lateral ties amongst companies via strategic alliances or the adoption of an economic development mission by universities.
2   The influence and interaction of one helix on another, for example, the role of government in setting overall economic policy influences both industry and universities.
3   The creation of new trilateral networks of universities, industry and government, for example, by creating regional economic clusters.
4   The effect of the Triple Helix on society over time, for example, on how the meaning and position of science is being developed.

The Entrepreneurial University

At the heart of the Triple Helix paradigm is the emergence of the so-called Entrepreneurial University. Traditionally universities had but two primary functions: To expand human knowledge via curiosity-driven research and to teach students. Universities were funded by the state but remained as largely autonomous institutions. Over the last 20 or so years there has been a shift in this model.

The demand for university education has dramatically increased so that in the UK, for example, around 50% of young people go to university, compared with fewer than 10% in the recent past. This expansion has been driven by the emergence of the post-industrial knowledge economy, with policymakers convinced that only nations with a strong graduate workforce will be able to compete in the future. This expansion has placed pressure on central funding, leading to the emergence of tuition fees and student loans.

Knowledge Management and Innovation 57

In parallel governments have increasingly viewed universities as instruments to drive a wide range of policy initiatives. For example, in the UK universities are now expected to:

- Develop graduate employability skills, such as team working, problem solving and communication skills, as well as develop the more traditional academic competencies, such as critical thinking and scientific enquiry.
- Provide a much stronger focus on teaching quality and student satisfaction, measured by increases in student contact hours, and by increasing the percentage of students who are awarded top degrees.
- Promote diversity, equality, inclusion and social mobility, for example, by reducing entrance requirements for disadvantaged students.
- Focus their research primarily on national industrial and business priorities rather than curiosity-driven research, that is, only research with a clearly defined economic benefit is deemed worthwhile.
- Commercialise their research and intellectual property through developing profit-making spin-out companies and science parks (therefore supplementing reductions in government funding).
- Be the catalysts and focal points for local economic regeneration and employment.

For Entrepreneurial Universities economic development has become a core mission. The Entrepreneurial University has moved from a generator of new knowledge to both a generator and commercialiser of new knowledge. In this way Entrepreneurial Universities embrace the spirit of commercial organisations whose interest in knowledge has always been closely tied to economic utility.

To a large extent the change required to transform a traditional university into an Entrepreneurial University is dependent on the collective attitudes and core beliefs of faculty members. For some, the naked dash for research commercialisation is a betrayal of the ideals that underpin the purpose of a university and an attack on academic freedom. For others, commercialising research is a natural extension of a university's mission, opening up opportunities to the benefit of the institution, the individual researcher, the wider economy and society.

Etzkowitz himself remains an energetic and charismatic focal point for the Triple Helix. Recently I had the opportunity of watching him deliver a keynote speech at a conference in which he convincingly made the case for the shifting mission of universities in directly driving innovation and economic development. Overall, the Triple Helix is an elegant and memorable term to describe university, industry and government interactions and to frame the research investigating this area.

User-Centred Innovation

As we saw in Chapter 4, a quote attributed to Henry Ford is that if he had asked his customers what they wanted, they would have said *"a faster horse."* His point was that customers often lack the insights and imagination to predict their future requirements, and therefore innovation is best left to the experts. However, what if Ford's customers had turned around and said, *"A low cost, reliable automobile powered by an efficient internal combustion engine"* and then started providing Ford with their own drawings of what this would look like? And what if Ford's customers continued to make their own customised modifications to his Model T, for example, by painting it a colour other than black? This alternative scenario is the basis of 'User-Centred Innovation', a key innovation model developed by MIT Professor Eric von Hippel.

Von Hippel captured his thinking on User-Centred Innovation in his 2005 book *Democratizing Innovation*. By democratization von Hippel simply means that the users of both products and services are able to innovate for themselves and are no longer reliant on being dictated to by firms pursuing traditional Manufacturing-Centred Innovation. The advantage of User-Centred Innovation is that users get exactly what they want by utilising their knowledge of how a product or service works in practice to customise and optimise performance. Furthermore, users are in a unique position to develop customised solutions through in-field experimentation and trial-and-error type methodologies. Von Hippel cites examples such as open-source software development, sports equipment and surgical equipment as areas where users have developed their own innovative products for their own use.

Lead Users

So, who exactly are these 'users'? Von Hippel proposes that users are either firms or individuals that expect to benefit from using a product or service. This is in contrast to 'manufacturers', who expect to profit from selling a product or service. It is therefore argued that because it is users who directly benefit from the utility of innovations they are in a unique position to optimise benefits, costs and functionality.

However, not all users are the same. Von Hippel characterises 'Lead Users' as being at the leading edge of the market and significantly ahead of the majority of users. These Lead Users will be at the forefront of innovation and will expect to gain high benefits from developing solutions to their needs.

Lead Users need to consider several factors before making an innovate-or-buy decision. These include:

- Is there an existing product in the marketplace that meets their needs?
- Do they have the time and funding to develop their own solution?
- Will the benefits of a custom solution outweigh the costs and risks of development?

Von Hippel argues that there is a growing trend for users developing their own customised solutions. He suggests that the actual act of innovating may also be intrinsically rewarding for users, as well as help infuse an innovative culture throughout user firms. He also notes that users tend to share information and knowhow without seeking to protect their intellectual property, so-called free revealing. This helps to reinforce the strength of user communities as well as increase the rate of innovation diffusion. This is particularly valuable where the innovation has a societal benefit, for example, medical and surgical tools and techniques or educational services.

Von Hippel conceptualises a system where in many sectors User-Centred Innovation and Manufacturing-Centred Innovation co-exist and are mutually reinforcing. Often manufacturers can produce low-cost, high-volume product platforms which then undergo customisation from users. And manufacturers themselves can cultivate a network of Lead Users to help inform their new product development strategy. In this way firms that identify and collaborate with Lead Users can develop and enhance their opportunities for innovation.

Innovation and entrepreneurship in action: Lego

Lego is one of the world's most recognised companies and has pioneered developing collaborative customer communities and Lead Users to drive innovation. Founded in 1932 in Denmark, Lego is best known for the colourful interlocking plastic bricks that are used as creative toys. Lego is now the world's largest toy company, with annual revenues over £3 billion and over 18,000 employees. This is all the more remarkable given the changing nature of the toy market, where Lego no longer just competes directly with traditional firms like Mattel but now has to contend with Sony's Playstation, Nintendo's Wii and Microsoft's Xbox, as well as Netflix, Facebook and Instagram.

Historically Lego had been a private and tightly controlled company, paying particular attention to protecting its intellectual property and designing new products that closely matched its core market and brand values. Children tended to play with Lego alone or in small groups, and eventually most would lose interest in their teens. In the late 1990s and early 2000s Lego experimented with products that would appeal to older users, such as Star Wars– and Harry Potter–themed sets, and more technical sets, such as Lego Mindstorms, that incorporated robotics and programming. Simultaneously the rise of the internet allowed Lego enthusiasts to connect with each other and form user groups to share their hobby. This presented Lego with an opportunity to utilise users within these groups to support the innovation process.

Connecting with user groups generated several benefits for Lego. Users could be involved in identifying new markets and trends, co-creating new products, trialling and improving prototype products and in some cases were even hired by Lego as full-time employees. This has led to new opportunities and insights for Lego, as well as reduced product development times and costs. In 2005 Lego launched its 'Ambassadors Program' to formally recognise key Lead Users and involve them in innovation in a more systematic manner. As Lego enthusiasts, ambassadors gain intrinsic satisfaction and motivation from their participation and role in shaping future products, but for larger programmes remuneration for their input is also available.

Inevitably the interface between user groups and Lego employees required some adjustment before it worked effectively. There was some initial scepticism that users with no formal design training or experience in the market could make a positive impact. In addition there was a concern that adult users would focus on developing products that were too complex for children. To overcome these issues Lego formed internal teams to review and approve initial user ideas before they were developed further. As both Lego and users became more used to working together common practices were developed to set mutual expectations and responsibilities.

In 2008 Lego launched a new online platform, 'Lego Cuusoo' (now known as 'Lego Ideas'), to facilitate collaboration by allowing users to upload designs, which can then be voted for by other users. This provides access to both new ideas and initial market research, with designs receiving more than 10,000 votes worldwide being considered for production. For successful products royalties of up to 1% are paid to the original designer. Overall, the development of collaborative user groups has yielded significant benefits to Lego and is now firmly embedded into their innovation process.

Discussion and reflection activity

1. How is knowledge managed within your organisation, and is knowledge codified, personalised or a combination of these?
2. Would your organisation benefit from collaborations with universities and government? What steps could be taken to set these up?
3. What are the characteristics of Entrepreneurial Universities, and should more UK universities adopt this approach?
4. What opportunities does your organisation have to benefit from User-Centred Innovation?
5. Who are your Lead Users, and how does your organisation identify and engage with them?
6. What aspects of Lego's approach for developing innovation through collaboration could your organisation adopt?

Recommended reading

Antorini, Y. M., Muniz, A. and Askildsen, T. (2012). Collaborating with Customer Communities: Lessons from the Lego Group. *MIT Sloan Management Review*, 53(3), 73–79.

Basadur, M. and Gelade, G. A. (2006). The Role of Knowledge Management in the Innovation Process. *Creativity and Innovation Management*, 15(1), 45–62.

Donate, M. J. and de Pablo, J. D. S. (2015). The Role of Knowledge-Orientated Leadership in Knowledge Management Practices and Innovation. *Journal of Business Research*, 68, 360–370.

Dzisah, J. and Etzkowitz, H. (2011). Triple Helix Circulation: The Heart of Innovation and Development. *International Journal of Technology Management and Sustainable Development*, 7(2), 101–115.

Elvekrok, I., Veflen, N., Nilsen, W. R. and Gausdal, A. H. (2018). Firm Benefits From Regional Triple-Helix Networks. *Regional Studies*, 52(9), 1214–1224.

Etzkowitz, H. and Leydesdorff, L. (2000). The Dynamics of Innovation: From National Systems and 'Mode 2' to a Triple Helix of University-Industry-Government Relations. *Research Policy*, 29(2), 109–123.

Hansen, M., Nohria, N. and Tierney, T. (1999). What's Your Strategy for Managing Knowledge? *Harvard Business Review*, 77(2), 106–116.

Hienerth, C., Lettl, C. and Keinz, P. (2013). Synergies Among Producer Firms, Lead Users, and User Communities: The Case of the LEGO Producer-User Ecosystem. *Journal of Product Innovation Management*, 31(4), 848–866.

Linton, J. D. (2018). DNA of the Triple Helix: Introduction to the Special Issue. *Technovation*, 76, 1–2.

Plessis, M. (2007). The Role of Knowledge Management in Innovation. *Journal of Knowledge Management*, 55(6), 49–57.

Schweisfurth, T. G. (2017). Comparing Internal and External Lead Users as Sources of Innovation. *Research Policy*, 46(1), 238–248.

Thomke, S. and von Hippel, E. (2002). Customers as Innovators: A New Way to Create Value. *Harvard Business Review*, 80(4), 74–81.

Tidd, J. and Trewhella, M. (1997). Organisational and Technological Antecedents for Knowledge Acquisition and Learning. *R&D Management*, 27(4), 359–375.

von Hippel, E. (2005). *Democratizing Innovation*. Cambridge, MA: MIT Press.

von Hippel, E. and Euchner, J. (2013). User Innovation. *Research Technology Management*, 56(3), 15–20.

6 Intellectual property and Open Innovation

Essential summary

1. The purpose of a patent is to protect the intellectual property that underpins new products or processes by granting a temporary monopoly for up to 20 years. For a patent to be granted a new invention must pass three tests:
   - **Novelty:** The invention must be new and not previously disclosed to the public before the date the patent is applied for.
   - **Inventiveness:** The invention must not be obvious or a minor modification or extension of what is already known.
   - **Industrial Application:** The invention must be deemed to make a positive technical contribution to industry, that is, it must demonstrate its practical usefulness.

2. The term 'Open Innovation' was established by Berkeley Professor Henry Chesbrough and is based on the view that valuable ideas and knowledge can come from outside a company, as well as from internal sources such as traditional R&D departments. Chesbrough argues that Open Innovation is distinctive from previous models of collaborative innovation, for example, through the proactive management of intellectual property, development of robust business models and utilisation of new metrics.

3. Open Innovation can be difficult to successfully implement, and the key barriers are 'Not-Invented-Here Syndrome' (NIH Syndrome) and a lack of 'Absorptive Capacity', defined as:

   Not-Invented-Here Syndrome is the tendency of a project group of stable composition to believe it possesses a monopoly of knowledge in its

> *field which leads it to reject ideas from outsiders, to the likely detriment of its performance.*
>
> *Absorptive Capacity is the ability of a firm to recognise the value of new, external information, assimilate it, and apply it to commercial ends.*

The particularly dangerous aspect of NIH Syndrome is that it often occurs at the subconscious level of decision-making, making it difficult to diagnose and overcome.

Intellectual property and patents

Innovation requires a significant investment in time and resources to create, develop and commercialise new technologies and products. In addition, firms must also accept the inherent risks associated with potential technological or market failure. However, the commercial rewards associated with successful innovation would be significantly reduced if competitors were free to launch their own copies into the marketplace, and this would be a disincentive for investment and risk taking by pioneers.

An overall reduction of innovation activity in markets and the wider economy would clearly be an unsatisfactory situation, and therefore governments have developed a legal framework to protect the 'intellectual property' of pioneers. Intellectual property can be broadly thought of as:

> *The ownership of intangible assets such as new ideas, concepts, names, designs and artistic works.*

There are broadly four methods of legally protecting intellectual property: copyright, trademarks, registered designs and patents.

Copyright, trademarks and registered designs

Copyright is an automatic right that protects the authors of an original work, such as writing, music or art, from unauthorised copying for up to 70 years after the originator's death. For example, this book is protected by copyright, so you can't make or distribute paper or electronic copies to third parties without breaking the law. Just thought I'd mention it.

Trademarks are words, logos, pictures, sounds, shapes or a combination of these elements that indicate the origin of goods or services. Registering a trademark (for a fee) allows you to stop others from using it without permission. Once granted trademarks must be renewed every ten years, but this can be done indefinitely.

Registered designs protect the appearance of a product from being copied, in particular its lines, contours, shape and texture. The design must be new and deemed to have individual character, but once this is established the protection lasts for up to 25 years subject to the payment of registration and renewal fees.

Patents

The purpose of a patent is to protect the intellectual property that underpins products or processes that utilise new technologies or have new functionalities. If a patent is granted by the Intellectual Property Office, it provides a temporary monopoly for the inventor in exchange for fully disclosing the invention. This monopoly usually has a duration of 20 years, or 15 years for medicines and pharmaceuticals. During this period the patent holder receives exclusive rights to exploit the invention by making and selling the product themselves, subcontracting manufacture and selling the product, licencing the patent rights in exchange for a royalty payment or by simply selling the patent rights to a third party. However, for a patent to be granted a new invention must pass three tests: novelty, inventiveness and industrial application.

Novelty: The invention must be new and not previously disclosed to the public before the date for which the patent is applied. This means it is vital not to disclose the invention to anyone apart from to your legal representatives, such as a patent attorney. So, if you have a flash of inspiration, keep it to yourself until you have filed your patent application.

Inventiveness: The invention must not be obvious or a minor modification or extension of what is already known. So, you can't patent a laptop with 15 USB ports.

Industrial Application: The invention must be deemed to make a positive technical contribution to industry, that is, it must demonstrate its practical usefulness.

In addition to satisfying these tests there are also certain ideas that cannot be patented:

- Scientific or mathematical discoveries, theories or methods. So, for example, Sir Isaac Newton couldn't have patented his laws of motion or theory of universal gravity.
- Literary, dramatic, musical or artistic works (but these are automatically covered by copyright).

- Methods of doing business (unless technological innovation is involved).
- Methods of medical treatment, diagnosis or surgery. For example, you can patent a novel artificial artery but not the surgical procedure required to fit it.
- Animal or plant varieties, for example, a new breed of dairy cow or type of wheat.
- Anything which is deemed to be against public policy or morality.

What are the disadvantages with patents? As stated, monopoly rights are only granted for either 20 or 15 years, after which rivals can copy the invention, details of which are now fully disclosed and publicly available. Firms therefore need to ensure that they commercialise and monetise the invention successfully and establish a dominant market position within this period. This can be an issue for industries such as pharmaceuticals, where the time taken for additional medical trials and regulatory approval after a patent has been granted can delay the commercial launch of new drugs and treatments.

Patents can also be expensive and time consuming. The process usually requires the services of a highly paid patent attorney, it can take up to four years for a patent to be granted and even then the patent will only cover the country of issue. Overseas or worldwide patent protection involves significant additional complexity and expenditure.

But perhaps the largest drawback of patents is that if the inventor feels their patent has been infringed by a competitor, they must pursue this through the civil courts at their own expense, with no guarantee of their complaint being upheld. A well-known example of this concerns James Dyson, the British inventor of the dual cyclone vacuum cleaner. Dyson was forced to defend a patent infringement by the American giant Hoover, eventually winning £4 million in damages. Of course, if Dyson had lost, he would have had to pay the legal bill himself, and possibly Hoover's as well.

Larger companies operating in technology-driven markets tend to place the patent at the heart of their intellectual property protection strategy, particularly if they undertake significant amounts of R&D. In fact, the annual number of patent applications filed is often used as a proxy to measure R&D effectiveness by both companies and policymakers (and in turn R&D effectiveness is often used as a proxy to measure innovation effectiveness, although in my view this is an over-simplistic metric).

Despite the limitations highlighted earlier, the patent system is still widely viewed as supporting and encouraging invention and innovation. However, could it be that the patent system may also act as a disincentive to invention and innovation? A recent phenomena attracting practitioner anxiety and academic interest is the emergence of so-called patent sharks or trolls. These are companies that hold large portfolios of patents with the specific aim of making money by aggressively extracting royalty payments from firms that they accuse of infringing their patents.

Research (e.g. Reitzig, Henkel, and Heath, 2007) has indicated that shark companies appear to be growing in both number and sophistication, ruthlessly pursuing their prey through the courts. The emergence of patent sharks places additional costs on companies engaging in technological innovation through increased due diligence requirements and also the costs of fighting and settling a case if they become prey. It may also instil a heightened sense of caution and risk aversion, stifling innovation for fear of future litigation.

Sharks, of course, argue that they are operating within the law and are doing nothing wrong. It remains to be seen whether legislation regarding patents is modified to discourage the sharks or whether they grow and continue to feed. What is clear is that the patent will remain the strongest form of intellectual property protection and continue to play a key role in the dynamics of innovation.

Developing Open Innovation models

The term 'Open Innovation' was established by Berkeley Professor Henry Chesbrough in 2002. It is based on the view that valuable ideas and knowledge can come from outside a company as well as from internal sources, such as traditional R&D departments. A good example of this view is found in the 2000 Annual Report from the pharmaceutical giant Merck, which states:

> *Merck accounts for about 1% of the biomedical research in the world. To tap into the remaining 99%, we must actively reach out to universities, research institutions and companies worldwide to bring the best technology and potential products into Merck. The cascade of knowledge flowing from biotechnology and the unravelling of the human genome—to name only two recent developments—is far too complex for any one company to handle alone.*

The issue of increased complexity across technology-based sectors is one of the key drivers for seeking external ideas and knowledge. According to Chesbrough, the 20th century model of vertically integrated companies with large internal R&D centres driving new product development has slowly given way to more collaborative and cost-effective ways of conducting research. Ever more specialised technology combined with the availability of private equity funding and flexible labour markets has seen the growth of small entrepreneurial start-up companies which are now conducting an increasing amount of research. This is in contrast to an overall decrease in the amount of research conducted by larger companies.

However, many would argue that external collaborations have always been sought by large research-intensive companies. For example, since 1990 the UK engineering group Rolls-Royce plc has formed around 30 formal collaborations with leading universities around the world. As long ago as 1988, Professor Eric von Hippel (who we came across in Chapter 5) identified seven sources of useful external knowledge companies use: suppliers, customers, universities, government research laboratories, private research laboratories, competitors (whose innovations can be imitated) and knowledge from other nations. Some scholars (e.g. Trott and Hartmann, 2009) have somewhat harshly criticised Open Innovation as just 'old wine in new bottles'.

Characteristics of Open Innovation

So, what is new about Open Innovation, and how does it represent a new paradigm in innovation strategy? Chesbrough argues that there is a combination of eight features which make Open Innovation distinctive from previous models of collaborative innovation:

1 Open Innovation is underpinned by a robust business model

A fundamental characteristic of Open Innovation is that value creation and value capture are driven by a robust business model designed to exploit the benefits of external ideas and knowledge. For many companies ideas and knowledge drawn from external sources are just adsorbed into the R&D department. Furthermore, the work conducted in traditional R&D departments is often only loosely tied to the company's business strategy. Companies that are successfully utilising Open Innovation have specifically changed their business model to maximise the benefits of external collaborations. For these companies Open Innovation is fully integrated into their business model, not just an initiative which makes a small contribution to competitiveness.

2 External ideas and knowledge are viewed as equal in value to internally generated ideas and knowledge

Companies that embrace Open Innovation view ideas and knowledge from external sources as equal in value to internally generated ideas and knowledge. These companies have overcome the widespread 'Not-Invented-Here Syndrome' in which external ideas and knowledge are viewed as low quality and inherently risky. Even if a company does engage with external collaborations, the benefits of these collaborations are likely to be severely restricted without first overcoming NIH Syndrome (see next section).

3 External ideas and knowledge are viewed as abundant

Traditional R&D-intensive companies believe ideas and knowledge are a scarce resource, and trying to find what you are looking for outside the company is like looking for a needle in a haystack. Far better to focus on internal resources because there is more chance of eventually generating what it is you are looking for. In contrast, companies that have successfully embraced Open Innovation not only believe that external ideas and knowledge are of equal value to internally generated ideas and knowledge but that they are also abundant and widely distributed. These companies therefore invest the time and resources to track down these external sources.

4 Outbound technology flows open up new markets

Traditional R&D-intensive firms seek external ideas and knowledge to supplement internal development, manufacture and sales. Companies adopting an Open Innovation business model utilise external ideas and knowledge to open up new markets for their existing technologies, particularly technologies which have not yet found a route to market. In this way external ideas and knowledge become market enablers, allowing companies to make larger returns on their technology investments.

5 Proactive intellectual property management

Traditional R&D-intensive companies employ intellectual property protection extensively, particularly through patents. Companies utilising an Open Innovation strategy are much more proactive in extracting the latent value from their intellectual property. For example, selling IP, licensing deals and even sharing, donating or publishing IP is employed if it will release future value.

6 Technology intermediaries are utilised

Companies adopting an Open Innovation strategy recognise the ever-increasing complexity of technology and the rapid pace of change. For these reasons they are likely to employ technology intermediaries to facilitate access to external ideas and knowledge. This is a particular trend in the pharmaceuticals sector but is growing across other sectors through intermediaries such as NineSigma and Innocentive.

7 Project evaluation focuses on making gains rather than avoiding losses

Many companies manage innovation as a process which utilises staged gates to filter R&D projects as they progress. These processes discard projects which do not fit the company's business model or strategic focus or projects which carry high perceived levels of risk. This risk has three components:

- Will the technology actually work?
- Will there be a market for it?
- Will I get the blame if something goes wrong?

In this way the innovation process is set up to filter out so-called type I errors, also known as false positives, that is, projects which are expected to succeed but fail commercially.

However, companies that adopt an Open Innovation strategy are also concerned with type II errors, false negatives. These are projects which were predicted to fail (and were therefore terminated) but actually would have succeeded. These companies take a much stronger line on avoiding missed opportunities, rather than being predominantly focused on filtering out risk.

8 Different metrics are used to measure Open Innovation

The final aspect which distinguishes Open Innovation as a new innovation model is the use of a different set of metrics to measure success. Traditional inwardly looking measures of innovation include:

- R&D spend as a percentage of sales.
- Number of patents as a percentage of R&D spend.
- Number of R&D employees.
- Percentage of 'new' products taken to market.

These metrics will still be important, but a new set of metrics will also be needed to manage Open Innovation, for example:

- Percentage of R&D conducted external to the firm.
- Rate of patent utilisation and income from technology licencing.
- Number of employees dedicated to external networks.
- Number of external networks and channels to market.

Overall, there is no doubt that the concept of Open Innovation has captured the imagination of both the research community and practitioners. I was fortunate to attend a keynote by Henry Chesbrough at a conference, where he made a convincing case for Open Innovation and its increased adoption. He noted that a Google search for the keywords 'open' and 'innovation' used to yield only a handful of results, usually concerning companies that had opened a centre for innovation. A Google search now gives over 500 million results!

Not-Invented-Here Syndrome and Absorptive Capacity

Open Innovation can be difficult to successfully implement, and the key barriers are 'Not-Invented-Here Syndrome' and a lack of 'Absorptive Capacity'. The first academic study of Not-Invented-Here Syndrome was made in 1967 by MIT Masters student Robert Clagett with his thesis entitled 'Receptivity to Innovation—Overcoming NIH'. Clagett studied eight cases of successful and unsuccessful implementations of process innovations developed in the R&D unit of a large US-based firm. He observed that the acronym NIH had been used by staff to describe the attitude of technical organisations that resist the adoption of innovations proposed from sources outside of the organisation.

Fifteen years later the study of NIH was revived by Professors Ralph Katz and Thomas Allen who introduced the phrase 'Not-Invented-Here Syndrome' and proposed the now widely accepted definition as:

> *The tendency of a project group of stable composition to believe it possesses a monopoly of knowledge in its field which leads it to reject ideas from outsiders, to the likely detriment of its performance.*

As the economies of the developed world continue to be driven by knowledge, organisations must increasingly look for external sources of ideas, knowledge and technology to complement their internal capabilities. To fail to do this puts the organisation at a significant competitive disadvantage, leading to eventual failure if the situation persists.

Characteristics of Not-Invented-Here Syndrome

A particularly dangerous aspect of NIH Syndrome is that it often occurs at the subconscious level of decision-making. This can make it difficult to diagnose and overcome. There are several explanations for why this may happen, including:

- General organisational resistance to any change in the familiar working environment which may generate additional levels of uncertainty or effort.

- Resistance to external technology due to the potential damage to the organisation's collective identity, for example, *"We are the leaders in Technology X, why do we need outsiders?"*
- A subconscious desire to reduce stress and insecurity in the working environment leads to routines and rigid roles in stable project teams, which reduce the openness to external ideas, knowledge and technology.
- Reward and incentive schemes which only encourage the development of internally generated ideas, knowledge and technology.
- Historical negative experiences with externally generated ideas, knowledge or technology leading to an overly cautious and sceptical mindset.
- External ideas, knowledge and technology are perceived as inherently higher risk than those generated internally and therefore are not pursued.
- External ideas, knowledge and technology are perceived as a threat to status and job security, particularly within the science, engineering, technology and R&D communities.
- Generally poor innovation strategy and leadership within the organisation leads to a lack of awareness of the benefits of seeking out external sources of ideas, knowledge and technology.

As can be readily appreciated, each of these is a significant barrier to implementing an Open Innovation model.

Absorptive Capacity

A major development in understanding organisational resistance to adopting external ideas came in 1990 with the publication of Wesley Cohen and Daniel Levinthal's influential paper 'Absorptive Capacity: A New Perspective on Learning and Innovation'. Absorptive Capacity is defined as:

> *The ability of a firm to recognise the value of new, external information, assimilate it, and apply it to commercial ends.*

Importantly, Cohen and Levinthal argue that the firm's existing level of knowledge (which may come from R&D or manufacturing expertise) underpins its ability to absorb external knowledge. So, in this respect external knowledge cannot be used to fully substitute internal knowledge but is instead complementary.

Clearly a firm's overall Absorptive Capacity will be strongly related to the Absorptive Capacity of its individual members, so careful consideration of employee recruitment and development policy is required. However, there are other steps that can be taken to enhance organisational Absorptive Capacity and reduce the influence of NIH Syndrome. These include:

- Ensuring project teams are regularly refreshed. Katz and Allen suggest that three years is about right and that NIH Syndrome can start to take hold after this point is reached.
- Ensuring internal knowledge–generating capability, for example R&D, remains strong to effectively assimilate external knowledge.
- Paying close attention to communication systems and boundary-spanning roles to ensure knowledge diffuses across organisational interfaces.
- Fostering a culture of continuous learning within the organisation through the development of problem-solving skills and capturing the lessons of past successes and failures.
- Recognising, rewarding and publicising successful projects that utilise both internal and external knowledge to reinforce the right organisational behaviours.

So, in summary, organisations should aim to avoid NIH Syndrome and increase their Absorptive Capacity to capitalise on external sources of ideas, knowledge and technology and to implement Open Innovation models.

Innovation and entrepreneurship in action: Xerox

Xerox is a major US corporation operating in the photocopying, printing and document-management markets. Founded in 1906 as the Haloid Photographic Company it changed its name to Xerox in 1961 following its development of the world's first commercial photocopying machine. Today Xerox employs some 140,000 staff and regularly posts revenues of $20 billion and operating profits of $1 billion. However, critics would point out that performance is relative, and Xerox's profits are dwarfed by companies such as Microsoft and Apple. They would also point out that while Microsoft and Apple founded their businesses on the back of the personal computer it was Xerox that actually invented, and then ignored, the PC.

In fact, the PC is one of a long line of innovations developed by Xerox but successfully commercialised by other players in the market. The source of Xerox's innovations is their Palo Alto Research Centre, or PARC for short. Nestling in the hills overlooking Silicon Valley, PARC was developed in the 1970s by Chief Executive Peter McColough. His vision was to establish a world-class R&D centre that would allow Xerox to become a dominant force in the new information age. PARC recruited the world's leading scientists who pioneered major breakthroughs.

However, it soon became clear that only the technology directly supporting Xerox's core photocopying business was being adopted, the rest being rejected by senior management at Xerox's Connecticut headquarters as too risky/unproven/expensive. This proved extremely frustrating for PARC's scientists, many of whom left to join other organisations or started their own businesses. Three examples that illustrate the problems associated with PARC are the development of the Xerox Alto, Ethernet and finally the Laser Printer.

Xerox Alto

Many consider the Xerox Alto as the first true personal computer. Developed in 1973 it was ahead of its time, featuring a cathode ray tube screen, a mouse-type control device, QWERTY keyboard and windows-type operating system, allowing users to open programmes and files by clicking onscreen icons. However, Xerox could not see its commercial potential, and its use was restricted to PARC itself and a few government contracts.

All this changed in 1979 when a certain Steve Jobs persuaded Xerox to give him a private tour of PARC. Once inside Jobs was immediately stunned by the Xerox Alto and could not believe that Xerox had not seen its enormous commercial potential. Jobs instructed his own team to replicate the Xerox Alto and quickly marketed his own Apple Lisa machine followed by the all-conquering Macintosh series. Meanwhile, Microsoft cleaned up on PC operating systems. Belatedly Xerox entered the market with their Xerox Star series of workstations, but by this time cheaper rivals were also entering the market and Xerox were eventually forced to accept defeat.

Ethernet

One of the pioneering features of the Xerox Alto was the development of the world's first working Ethernet to link up machines, including an early version of email. This was quite handy because it allowed PARC scientists to exchange data and communicate with each other efficiently. But what about the commercial potential? Ethernet connectivity soon became embedded in Xerox products, allowing a variety of equipment configurations to be joined with a single cable. However, Xerox could not see any applications beyond this and was happy to grant the inventor of Ethernet, Robert Metcalfe, a license to exploit the technology for a token one-off fee of just $1,000.

Metcalfe had by this time already left Xerox and teamed up with Digital Equipment Corporation (DEC) and chip giant Intel to develop a Technology

Standard based around his Ethernet protocol. Metcalfe quickly secured venture capital funding and launched his own company, 3Com, to take Ethernet technology to the mass market. 3Com eventually went public in 1984, at one point surpassing the value of Xerox itself, before eventually being bought by HP for $2.7 billion in 2009.

Laser printer

One of the problems with both the Xerox Alto and Ethernet technology was that they were seen as outside of Xerox's core product portfolio. But what about printing? Surely copying and printing were strategically aligned? Certainly that's what PARC scientist Gary Starkweather thought when he conceived the world's first laser printer. This could even be incorporated into a Xerox photocopier, giving users the ability to both copy and print documents directly from a computer.

Starkweather unveiled his laser printer in 1969, but once Xerox's management saw what it was capable of they were unsupportive, perhaps concerned that high-quality on-demand printing would render their copiers obsolete. So, the laser printer was mothballed—until IBM launched their own in 1976. This prompted Xerox to finally launch their own competing 9700 model the following year. Laser printing has eventually gone on to become a multibillion-dollar business for Xerox, vindicating Starkweather.

Yet despite these missed opportunities Xerox has resisted Schumpeter's *creative destruction* and are still going; so, the question shifts from 'What if?' to 'What now?' Harvard professors Scott Anthony and Clayton Christensen suggest in their excellently titled 2012 paper 'The Empire Strikes Back' that developing disruptive services under the leadership of CEO Ursula Burns is paying dividends for Xerox. Facilitated by the 2009 acquisition of Affiliated Computer Services for $6.4 billion, services are expected to account for two-thirds of Xerox's future revenues. So, it appears business model innovation will play as much a part in Xerox's future as product innovation and technology development have in the past.

Discussion and reflection activity

1. How does your organisation protect its intellectual property?
2. Do patents stimulate or hinder innovation in large organisations? What about for start-ups and SMEs? What about for your organisation?
3. How could your organisation develop its external network to drive innovation?

4 What might the organisational barriers and strategic risks associated with implementing Open Innovation be for your organisation? How could these be overcome?
5 Are there examples of NIH Syndrome from within your organisation? What was the impact? How could NIH Syndrome be overcome?
6 What factors do you think led to the failure of Xerox to successfully commercialise the technology developed at PARC?

Recommended reading

Anthony, S. and Christensen, C. (2012). The Empire Strikes Back: How Xerox and Other Large Corporations are Harnessing the Force of Disruptive Innovation. *Technology Review*, 115(1), 66–24.

Antons, D. and Piller, F. (2015). Opening the Black Box of 'Not Invented Here' Attitudes, Decision Biases, and Behavioural Consequences. *Academy of Management Perspectives*, 29(2), 193–217.

Candelin-Palmqvist, H., Sandberg, B. and Mylly, U. (2012). Intellectual Property Rights in Innovation Management Research: A Review. *Technovation*, 32(9/10), 502–512.

Chesbrough, H. W. (2003). The Era of Open Innovation. *MIT Sloan Management Review*, 44(3), 35–41.

Chesbrough, H. W. (2007). Why Companies Should Have Open Business Models. *MIT Sloan Management Review*, 48(2), 22–28.

Chesbrough, H. W. (2017). The Future of Open Innovation. *Research Technology Management*, 60(1), 35–38.

Cohen, W. and Levinthal, D. (1990). Absorptive Capacity: A New Perspective on Learning and Innovation. *Administrative Science Quarterly*, 35, 128–32.

Grimaldi, M., Greco, M. and Cricelli, L. (2021). A Framework of Intellectual Property Protection Strategies and Open Innovation. *Journal of Business Research*, 123, 156–164.

Hannen, J., Antons, D., Piller, F., Salge, T., Coltman, T. and Devinney, T. M. (2019). Containing the Not-Invented-Here Syndrome in External Knowledge Absorption and Open Innovation: The Role of Indirect Countermeasures. *Research Policy*, 48(9). https://doi.org/10.1016/j.respol.2019.103822.

Hussinger, K. and Wastyn, A. (2016). In Search for the Not-Invented-Here Syndrome: The Role of Knowledge Sources and Firm Success. *R&D Management*, 46(53), 945–947.

Pisano, G. and Teece, D. (2007). How to Capture Value from Innovation: Shaping Intellectual Property and Industry Architecture. *California Management Review*, 50(1), 278–296.

Reitzig, M., Henkel, J. and Heath, C. (2007). On Sharks, Trolls, and Their Patent Prey—Unrealistic Damage Awards and Firms' Strategies of 'Being Infringed'. *Research Policy*, 36(1), 134–154.

Schweisfurth, T. G. and Raasch, C. (2018). Absorptive Capacity for Need Knowledge: Antecedents and Effects for Employee Innovativeness. *Research Policy*, 47(4), 687–699.

Trott, P. and Hartmann, D. (2009). Why 'Open Innovation' is Old Wine in New Bottles. *International Journal of Innovation Management*, 13(4), 715–736.

Zahra, M. and George, G. (2002). Absorptive Capacity: A Review, Reconceptualization, and Extension. *Academy of Management Review*, 27, 185–203.

7 Disruptive innovation and technology management

Essential summary

1. Harvard Professor Clayton Christensen defined 'Disruptive Innovation' as:

   An innovation that helps create a new market and eventually disrupts an existing market, often by displacing an earlier technology.

   This contrasts with 'Sustaining Innovation', defined as:

   An innovation that does not create new markets, but enables firms to compete more effectively by offering improvements to existing products or services.

   Christensen argues that good management practice, such as staying close to customers, developing new products and services to precisely to meet their needs and focusing on maximising prices, profits and share price, can all make a company vulnerable to the threat of game-changing competitors with Disruptive Innovations.

2. The 'S-Curve' model shows how R&D investment in developing a technology can lead to improvements in performance before diminishing returns set in and switching to a new technology is required to achieve further performance improvement. The timing of this switch is crucial. Switching too soon means the opportunity to develop useful improvements to the existing technology is lost. Switching too late may leave firms at a competitive disadvantage to firms that made the switch earlier.

3. The central role of a technological 'Standard' is to provide compatibility between products and their interfaces. This interconnectivity is particularly important when considering product-to-human interfaces, where

tacit knowledge relating to the Standard quickly diffuses throughout the market. A Standard is usually specific to the firm that created it and can lead to 'Standard Wars' between rival firms to establish market dominance.

In contrast, a 'Dominant Design' is the result of an industry-wide evolution of a product or class of products that eventually incorporates a range of design features and attributes the market comes to expect. A Dominant Design represents the industry's convergence on an accepted product architecture that once established becomes relatively stable over an extended period of time.

Disruptive Innovation

What do the bow and arrow, the sailing ship and the compact disc all have in common? They have all been superseded by new disruptive technologies that have had a global impact (gunpowder, propeller propulsion systems and internet downloads). Harvard Professor Clayton Christensen's research on Disruptive Innovation is one of the cornerstones of innovation management, exploring how organisations can both seize opportunities to disrupt existing markets and avoid falling victim to Disruptive Innovation themselves.

Christensen first considered disruption in his 1995 Harvard Business Review paper 'Disruptive Technologies: Catching the Wave', co-authored with Joseph Bower. His breakthrough came two years later with the publication of the book *The Innovator's Dilemma*. In the book Christensen focuses on 'disruptive technology', although his later work on business growth replaces this with the term 'Disruptive Innovation', defined as:

> *An innovation that helps create a new market and eventually disrupts an existing market, often by displacing an earlier technology.*

Christensen distinguishes Disruptive Innovation from what he terms 'Sustaining Innovation', defined as:

> *An innovation that does not create new markets, but enables firms to compete more effectively by offering improvements to existing products or services.*

Sustaining Innovations are mainly small, incremental improvements to existing products or services. However, they can also be more ambitious in scope, delivering breakthroughs in performance and allowing the firm to charge higher prices. In contrast, Disruptive Innovations are often simpler, more convenient and lower-priced products or services, which appeal to new or less-demanding customers. But once the Disruptive Innovation gains traction in the market it becomes rapidly developed, appealing to more demanding customers. It can therefore be appreciated that Disruptive Innovation can be an opportunity for new firms but a significant threat for incumbents.

New technology per se is not necessarily disruptive. Christensen gives the example of the first automobiles, which did not disrupt the transportation market because they were so expensive that only the very wealthy could afford them. However, the Ford Model T was a Disruptive Innovation because it was the first affordable automobile, therefore it disrupted the global transportation market. Henry Ford's development of the efficient production line for assembly operations dramatically reduced the cost. Simultaneously Ford paid his workers a high (for the time) $5 per day, ensuring that they could afford to buy the Model T, therefore rapidly developing the adoption of this Disruptive Innovation.

So, now that we understand the distinction between Disruptive and Sustaining Innovation it should be relatively straightforward to manage them effectively. Unfortunately, it's not that simple! According to Christensen, the dilemma innovators face is that the failure to spot the opportunities and threats posed by Disruptive Innovations can be caused by the organisation's pursuit of good management practices. Christensen argues that good management practices, such as staying close to customers, developing new products and services to precisely to meet their needs and focusing on maximising prices, profits and share price, can all make a company vulnerable to the threat of game-changing competitors with Disruptive Innovations.

Let's take just one of these elements—staying close to the customer. This makes a lot of sense because without customers you have no sales, no profits and no business. However, customers are often not the best people to anticipate or express how new technology can better meet their future needs. For example, I happened to grow up when vinyl records were being replaced by compact discs, which were smaller, more resistant to scratches and jumping and didn't need to be turned over to play side B. Best of all, you could skip straight to your favourite songs at the press of a button. However, if at the time you had asked me what new music technology I wanted, I would have said *"A CD which is even more scratch resistant and has the capacity to store more songs."* I don't think that in 1990 I would have said, *"Download exactly the songs I want from the internet onto my smartphone for a fraction of the current price."*

So, for both CD manufacturers and the music industry in general staying close to the customer didn't help them to capitalise on new disruptive technology. Instead companies like Napster, Apple and Spotify, to name but three, were the ones to profit through disruption of the market. This is not an isolated case. Witness Kodak's failure to respond to the opportunities presented by digital photography or IBM's failure to move from mainframes into personal computers or indeed to spot that software would become more valuable than hardware—a fact not lost on a certain Bill Gates.

So, given the difficulty associated with Disruptive Innovation what advice can be offered to practicing managers? Christensen's research has indicated that the following approaches can help:

- Determine early on whether a new technology has the potential to be disruptive or will be sustaining only. This is the first step, and although most organisations have processes to identify and manage Sustaining Innovation not many focus on identifying and managing Disruptive Innovation.
- Don't measure the potential impact of a Disruptive Innovation with the same metrics used to assess Sustaining Innovation. For example, Sustaining Innovations always give an improvement in performance. By contrast, Disruptive Innovations are often initially associated with reduced performance and lower initial profits but with the potential to create or access new markets.
- Locate the initial market for the Disruptive Innovation. The classic example is the transistor, a technology which only became a global success once a low-cost mass-market application was identified—the transistor radio. Once this was established the transistor replaced vacuum tube technology in other electronic applications, rapidly making tubes obsolete.
- Separate responsibility for developing disruptive technologies from the mainstream business and keep it independent. This ensures that the disruptive business has dedicated resources and focus and is not tied to the same short-term profit targets of the mainstream business.
- Consider developing disruptive capabilities through acquisitions. For example, in the 1990s Cisco Systems expanded its capabilities quickly and cost effectively through a series of early-stage company acquisitions. It was therefore able to compete effectively with companies that had far more established internal technology development capabilities.
- Develop disruptive business models. For example, Ryanair used a low-cost business model to disrupt the European airline market. Dell used a mass customisation online business model to disrupt the global market for personal computers. Amazon used an online marketplace and warehouse distribution to disrupt traditional retailers.

Technological discontinuities and the S-Curve model

Over time technologies eventually become obsolete and are replaced, as demonstrated by the demise of magnetic tapes, piston-driven aero-engines, dot matrix printers, black-and-white TVs and dial-up internet. Given this, why is it that so many established companies seem to miss the opportunity to jump in time to catch the next wave of technological innovation and instead yield market share to their rivals? A key model that has emerged to map the progress and eventual replacement of technologies is the S-Curve. Like most good models the S-Curve is simple, powerful and easy to draw (see Figure 7.1).

The Y axis shows an appropriate measure of performance for the technology under consideration. For example, fuel economy is a useful measure of performance for aircraft gas turbine engines because it is valued by customers. Similarly, temperature capability is a good measure of the performance of turbine blades, because a higher temperature turbine gives a more fuel-efficient engine. The X axis measures the R&D effort required to improve the performance of the technology. R&D effort is usually measured as either cumulative R&D spend or time in years for industries with a steady rate of R&D expenditure.

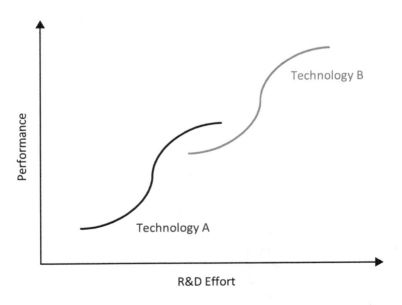

Figure 7.1 S-Curve

When a new technology is first introduced additional R&D effort leads to fairly modest improvements in performance, represented by the gradually rising lower portion of the S-Curve. However, as the technology becomes better understood increases in R&D generate greater returns in performance, represented by the mid-portion of the S-Curve. This is the period of technology development where a high level of performance improvement is achieved for a given level of R&D effort.

However, at some stage the technology starts to mature, and a point of inflection is reached where additional R&D investments generate reduced levels of performance improvement, or what economists would call 'diminishing returns'. Eventually no amount of additional R&D spend can improve performance as the natural limits of the technology are reached, shown by a flattening at the top of the S-Curve. At this point further performance gains can only be achieved by jumping to a new emerging technology that is in the early stages of its own S-Curve. The gap between Technology A and Technology B is often termed a 'discontinuity'.

Of course wise firms will not wait until their technology is obsolete before making the switch to the emerging technology. In this way the S-Curve can be used as a strategic tool to predict when the limits of a technology are likely to be reached and when to make the switch. But unfortunately technology development is not that straightforward, and companies can fall into three major traps:

1 Premature switching

This occurs when companies interpret the S-Curve data as showing that the technology is approaching maturity. They then switch to a new technology to generate further improvements in performance. However, technology development is not always predictable, and in the case of premature switching further significant performance gains could have been achieved by persevering with the original technology. By switching prematurely the company has missed out on the opportunity to extend the life of the original technology and has instead taken on the risk and considerable expense of developing a new technology and incorporating this into their products and manufacturing operations.

2 Delayed switching

The second trap arises when companies interpret the S-Curve data as showing that significant further improvements in performance are possible, but the reality is that technological obsolescence is fast approaching. In this situation they need to make a switch to an emerging technology that offers future performance levels beyond what can be achieved by persevering with the current technology. But their delay in making the switch allows competitors who have already made the switch the opportunity to achieve technological and performance leadership.

There are many reasons why companies fall into the delayed switching trap. There may be significant levels of risk aversion within the organisation, and power and politics may also play a strong role in persisting with a mature technology. For example, many magnetic tape manufacturers were slow to spot the potential for compact disc technology. The reason? Senior managers had built their reputations on the earlier development and commercialisation of magnetic tapes and were therefore not keen to embrace a new technology.

3 Performance myopia

The third trap is to focus on improving one particular performance characteristic at the component or sub-system level and failing to appreciate that overall product performance may be highly dependent on additional factors, including the overall architecture of the product. As an example, let's consider gas turbine aero-engine turbine blades. There is no doubt that increasing the temperature capability of the turbine blade material will improve overall engine efficiency and hence fuel economy. For this reason great improvements have been made in nickel superalloy materials technology, from refinements in alloy chemistry to the development of unidirectional grain structures and finally to the emergence of single-crystal blade technology. Each development is the result of extensive R&D and has resulted in increased temperature capability.

However, improved temperature capability can also be achieved by the development of a parallel technology, ceramic thermal barrier coatings. These allow the turbine blades to operate in environments well above the melting point of the nickel superalloy from which they are made. A technology strategy based solely on the development of improved nickel superalloys would not have achieved such a result. Similarly, temperature capability is only one determinant of overall engine efficiency. Designers also need to consider factors such as aerodynamic improvements, lightweight materials and novel engine architecture. So, for complex products a disproportionate focus on developing a single technology S-Curve is unlikely to deliver the optimum improvement in overall performance.

Having pointed out these traps you are probably questioning just how useful the S-Curve model is as a practical management tool. As a predictive model to precisely indicate when a technology will become obsolete and when firms should switch to a new technology it has its limits. But then again, can any tool deliver an accurate predictive capability? As Nobel physicist Niels Bohr once remarked, "*Prediction is difficult—especially if it's about the future!*" Perhaps the value of the S-Curve model is that it forces us to think carefully about the way technologies develop, become obsolete and get replaced and how this needs to be incorporated into corporate, product and R&D strategies. Companies using the S-Curve model might not always get this right, but at least they are actively considering the strategic options available.

Technology standards and dominant designs

Let's start this section with a short example concerning the development of the typewriter and the adoption of the QWERTY keyboard. The story begins in 1868 when the American inventor Christopher Latham Sholes was awarded a patent for the typewriter. Unfortunately, it still required significant development to overcome several technical problems. Chief amongst them was the persistent jamming of the type bars. As an attempt to overcome this problem Sholes experimented with the arrangement of the keys to reduce the likelihood of adjacent keys being hit in quick succession, eventually settling on the QWERTY pattern. The QWERTY arrangement was not concerned with improving typing speed, and indeed actively slowing down typing speed may also have been an aim, as this also helped avoid jams.

Sholes eventually sold the rights to his patent in 1873 to the established small arms manufacturer E. Remington & Sons. They used their engineering capability to make further mechanical improvements and then began production on a commercial scale. Gradually the typewriter with its QWERTY key arrangement became widely adopted, supported by the development of touch-typing techniques that improved typing speed. Typewriter salesmen also liked the QWERTY arrangement because they could quickly punch out the word 'typewriter' to sceptical prospective clients using only keys from the top row.

However, the fact remained that the QWERTY keyboard was not optimised for speed, and the mechanical jamming problem had long since been overcome. Surely then there would be a market for a keyboard optimised for typing speed that would soon make QWERTY obsolete? And that's exactly what American academic August Dvorak thought, patenting his Dvorak Simplified Keyboard (DSK) in 1936.

The DSK arrangement claimed greater typing speed and reduced typist fatigue, backed by the results of US Navy trials. However, despite these advantages the DSK failed to displace QWERTY, and after many years of fruitless effort Dvorak eventually died a bitter man. QWERTY had become the industry Standard, and the market did not perceive that DSK offered sufficient improvements to become a new Standard. For the English language, QWERTY remains the preferred keyboard layout to this day, even on tablet devices with touch screens.

Standard Wars

The chances of successfully developing an industry Standard can potentially be enhanced by adopting a 'First Mover Advantage' strategy (see Chapter 8), particularly if the intellectual property is protected by patents (see Chapter 6). However, rival Standards are often developed simultaneously, leading to so-called Standard Wars—battles for market dominance between incompatible technologies. Perhaps the most famous example of a Standard War was the rivalry in the home video market between Sony's Betamax system and JVC's VHS system.

Sony developed the Betamax video system in the 1970s, offering a licence to rival JVC. However, instead of accepting the licence deal JVC launched their own competing 'Video Home System', or VHS for short. VHS was characterised by reduced costs at the expense of slightly inferior picture and sound quality. Crucially, the two systems were incompatible—a Betamax video cassette could not be played on a VHS video recorder and vice-versa. Price-conscious consumers started to side with VHS, and as their market share increased JVC enjoyed economies of scale; their costs (and prices) fell further, and the writing was on the wall for Sony.

Sony did not make the same mistake twice. When DVD technology replaced video, Sony bet the farm on their 'Blu-Ray' system becoming the Standard over Toshiba's rival 'HD DVD' system. Sony achieved early economies of scale by incorporating Blu-Ray into their own PlayStation games console. Eventually Blu-Ray prevailed as film distributors such as Warner Bros. lost patience with incurring the costs associated with supporting two formats and sided with Blu-Ray.

Dominant Designs

The concept of 'Dominant Designs' can be attributed to the seminal work of MIT Professor James Utterback and the late Harvard Professor Bill Abernathy. Standards and Dominant Designs are closely related, and indeed the two terms are often used interchangeably by managers, engineers and even some scholars. However, there are some important differences that once appreciated enable us to gain a more detailed understanding of the complex dynamics associated with developing new technologies, products and markets.

As we have seen in the earlier examples, the central role of Standards is to provide compatibility between products and their interfaces. This interconnectivity is particularly important when considering product-to-human interfaces, such as the QWERTY keyboard, where tacit knowledge relating to the Standard quickly diffuses throughout the market. A Standard is usually specific to the firm that created it and is established either before or in parallel with the product-development process.

In contrast to Standards, a Dominant Design is the result of an industry-wide evolution of a product or class of products that eventually incorporates a range of design features and attributes that the market comes to expect as 'standard' (so you can see where the terminology confusion creeps in). A Dominant Design represents the industry's convergence on an accepted product architecture that once established becomes relatively stable over an extended period of time.

A good example of a Dominant Design is the development of the automobile. In 1771 Frenchman Nicholas-Joseph Cugnot test drove the very first automobile, powered by a steam engine. Perhaps surprisingly steam engines were still used right up until the 1900s, but by this time electric and petrol-powered automobiles had also been developed by firms such as the Olds Motor Vehicle Company and the Daimler Motor Company.

Eventually the petrol- powered automobile became the accepted Dominant Design adopted by the industry's major players, such as Ford and General Motors. The petrol-powered (or diesel-powered) automobile has remained a Dominant Design over 100 years later, its efficiency and reliability steadily improved by a century of innovation. It is only relatively recently that electric vehicles are gaining market share, mainly spurred through governmental requirements to reduce greenhouse gas emissions and improve air quality.

Innovation and entrepreneurship in action: Dyson

Innovator, entrepreneur and billionaire Sir James Dyson has built his fortune on the development of 'dual cyclone' technology to improve the performance of the humble vacuum cleaner. His company employs over 12,000 people and has revenues in excess of £4 billion, and Dyson himself topped the Sunday Times Rich list in 2020 with a net worth of over £16 billion. However, his story is also one of setbacks, disappointments and decades of persistence in the face of adversity.

Dyson studied at the Royal College of Art before embarking on a career as an industrial designer in the 1970s. One of his notable inventions was the 'Ballbarrow', a wheelbarrow that used a ball instead of a wheel for enhanced manoeuvrability. Part of the production process involved spraying metal parts with epoxy powder, and Dyson investigated the use of industrial cyclone extraction technology similar to that used in sawmills to remove excess powder from the factory. At the same time Dyson also noticed that the suction performance of his Hoover domestic vacuum cleaner reduced as the dust bag became full. For Dyson this presented a potential opportunity. What if industrial cyclone extraction technology could be adapted for domestic vacuum cleaners, giving constant suction performance and removing the need for dust bags?

To answer this question Dyson embarked on a series of experiments, and after five years of work and some 5,127 prototypes Dyson finally revealed his 'G-Force' design in 1983. His plan was to licence the technology to existing vacuum cleaner manufacturers, such as Hoover, and then have a well-earned break as the royalty fees rolled in. But despite his confidence in the utility of his technology, one by one he was rejected by the established firms. They were unconvinced that customers would pay more for a constant suction vacuum cleaner. In addition, the vacuum cleaner bag market in the UK was worth an estimated £100 million per year, so Dyson's bagless technology was seen as a threat to revenues rather than an asset.

Undeterred Dyson licenced the G-Force in 1985 to a Japanese company, Apex Ltd, and launched in Japan with a distinctive pink colour and a premium price of over £1,000. This was successful and allowed Dyson to set up his own manufacturing operations in the UK in 1991, launching a series of dual cyclone models and capturing a significant share of the domestic vacuum cleaner market in the UK and the United States. This did not go unnoticed by the major manufacturers, and in 1999 Hoover launched its 'triple vortex' competitor. Dyson promptly sued for patent infringement, and in 2000 at the Royal Courts of Justice in London judges found in Dyson's favour, awarding £4 million in damages. The irony that Hoover was one of the companies Dyson originally approached to licence his dual cyclone technology was not lost on anyone.

Since then Dyson has gone from strength to strength and developed new product lines, including efficient hand dryers, bladeless fans and air purifiers, hair straighteners and LED lamps. Developments in washing machine and electric vehicle technology have been less successful, despite investing £500 million in the latter. But Dyson himself is undaunted, stating:

> *Since day one we have taken risks and dared to challenge the status quo with new products and technologies. Such an approach drives progress, but has never been an easy journey—the route to success is never linear. I remain as excited about the future of Dyson as I have always been.*

Discussion and reflection activity

1 What Disruptive Innovation opportunities and threats apply to your business sector?
2 How could your organisation identify and manage Disruptive Innovations more effectively?
3 How could the S-Curve model be applied to your organisation?
4 What Standards and Dominant Designs apply to your business sector?
5 What factors have underpinned Sir James Dyson's success?
6 Is Dyson's dual cyclone vacuum cleaner a Disruptive Innovation or a Sustaining Innovation? Why?

Recommended reading

Anderson, P. and Tushman, M. L. (1990). Technological Discontinuities and Dominant Designs: A Cyclical Model of Technology Change. *Administrative Science Quarterly*, 35, 604–633.

Bergek, A., Berggren, C., Magnusson, T. and Hobday, M. (2013). Technological Discontinuities and the Challenge for Incumbent Firms: Destruction, Disruption or Creative Accumulation? *Research Policy*, 42(6/7), 1210–1224.

Bower, J. L. and Christensen, C. (1995). Disruptive Technologies: Catching the Wave. *Harvard Business Review*, 73(1), 43–53.

Brem, A., Nylund, P. A. and Schuster, G. (2016). Innovation and De Facto Standardization: The Influence of Dominant Design on Innovative Performance, Radical Innovation, and Process Innovation. *Technovation*, 50(51), 79–88.

Christensen, C. M. (1992). Exploring the Limits of the Technology S-Curve. Part I: Component Technologies. *Production and Operations Management*, 1(4), 334–357.

Christensen, C. M., McDonald, R., Altman, E. J. and Palmer, J. E. (2018). Disruptive Innovation: An Intellectual History and Directions for Future Research. *Journal of Management Studies*, 55(7), 1043–1078.

Christensen, C., Johnson, M. and Rigby, D. (2002). Foundations for Growth: How to Identify and Build Disruptive New Businesses. *MIT Sloan Management Review*, 43(3), 22–31.

Christensen, C., Raynor, R. and McDonald, R. (2015). What is Disruptive Innovation? *Harvard Business Review*, 93(12), 44–53.

Danneels, E. (2004). Disruptive Technology Reconsidered: A Critique and Research Agenda. *Journal of Product Innovation Management*, 21(4), 246–258.

Gallagher, S. (2007). The Complementary Role of Dominant Designs and Industry Standards. *IEEE Transactions on Engineering Management*, 54(2), 371–379.

King, A. and Baatartogtokh, B. (2015). How Useful is the Theory of Disruptive Innovation? *MIT Sloan Management Review*, 57(1), 77–90.

Narayanan, V. K. and Chen, T. (2012). Research on Technology Standards: Accomplishment and Challenges. *Research Policy*, 41(8), 1375–1406.

O'Reilly, C. and Binns, A. J. M. (2019). The Three Stages of Disruptive Innovation: Idea Generation, Incubation, and Scaling. *California Management Review*, 61(3), 49–71.

Suarez, F. (1999). Battles for Technological Dominance: An Integrative Framework. *Research Policy*, 33, 271–286.

Utterback, J. M. (1995). Dominant Designs and the Survival of Firms. *Strategic Management Journal*, 16(6), 415–430.

8 Strategic innovation management

Essential summary

1. Firms must focus on concurrently managing three timelines, referred to as the 'three Horizons of growth'. Horizon 1 encompasses the current products, services and markets in which the firm competes. Even when these markets appear mature, continuing innovation can extend their growth and profitability. Horizon 2 encompasses fast-moving entrepreneurial ventures within the business which have the potential to rapidly grow and over time will replace current businesses. Horizon 3 encompasses long-term future opportunities. Although most of these embryonic businesses will not be successful, some will have the potential to become at least as profitable as the current core businesses.
2. Products and technologies have their own distinct life cycle, presented as a plot of annual market revenues against time. At the start of the product life cycle a new technology fights for market acceptance before experiencing a growth phase, then maturity, decline and finally obsolescence as it is replaced by another technology that offers the market greater utility. Managing product life cycles strategically presents a significant challenge to organisations. For example, the capabilities required to develop and launch a new product are much different than those required to maintain high sales in a mature market. Firms therefore need to adapt and align their innovation strategy with specific stages of the product life cycle.
3. The decision on whether to be a technology leader or technology follower is a major strategic consideration, and research has shown that there are both First Mover Advantages and First Mover Disadvantages.

    First Mover Advantages:
    - Technological leadership through the learning curve and patents.
    - Pre-emption of scarce assets.
    - Buyer switching costs.

Strategic innovation management

First Mover Disadvantages:

- Free rider effects.
- Technological and market uncertainty.
- Shifts in technology or customer needs.

The strength of the First Mover Advantage concept is that it forces firms to actively consider how innovation integrates with the wider business and commercial strategy of the firm.

Developing innovation Horizons

Horizons is a management framework first proposed by McKinsey & Company consultants Mehrdad Baghai, Stephen Coley and David White in their 2000 book *The Alchemy of Growth*. As the title suggests, they view sustained business growth as an elusive goal for most firms. This is because the focus on managing the present limits investment in future products, services and markets—a theme also addressed in the Organisational Ambidexterity literature we considered in Chapter 4.

The Horizons model argues that as a firm's business and revenue streams mature it must have new streams ready to take their place and that to sustain growth there must be a continuous pipeline of new sources of profit. The pipeline is segmented into mature, emergent and embryonic phases of the business life cycle, referred to as the 'three Horizons of growth'.

Horizon 1

This encompasses the current products, services and markets in which the firm competes. Even when these markets appear mature, continuing innovation can extend their growth and profitability, particularly when combined with efforts to improve operational efficiency and reduce costs. When considering Horizon 1, managers should ask themselves:

- Are our core businesses generating sufficient profits to allow us to invest in growth?
- Can performance and profits be pushed higher over the next few years?
- Is our cost structure competitive with the rest of the industry?
- Are we protected from new competitors, technologies and regulations which could disrupt the market?

Horizon 2

This encompasses fast-moving entrepreneurial ventures within the business which have the potential to rapidly grow but not without a significant investment in company resources. Horizon 2 is about building new streams of revenue which over time will replace current businesses. A growth-focused company needs to develop several of these emerging businesses concurrently to mitigate the risk of market failure. When considering Horizon 2, managers need to ask themselves:

- Do we have new businesses capable of creating as much value as the current core businesses?
- Are these new businesses gaining momentum in the marketplace?
- Are we prepared to make substantial investments to accelerate their growth?
- Are these new businesses attracting the entrepreneurial talent in our organisation?
- Do we need to access or acquire new capabilities from external sources?

Horizon 3

This encompasses long-term future opportunities. These are more than just ideas; they must consist of real activities, testing, trials and small investments. Although the majority of these embryonic businesses will not be successful, they need to be promising enough that some of them will go on to succeed in becoming at least as profitable as the current core businesses. When considering Horizon 3, managers need to ask themselves:

- Does our top leadership team devote sufficient time to consider long-term growth opportunities?
- Have we developed a portfolio of options for reinventing existing businesses and creating new ones?
- Are we developing effective ways to turn these ideas into new businesses?
- Have the ideas been made tangible with measurable first steps?

The key to achieving sustainable growth is to manage Horizons 1, 2 and 3 concurrently. The Horizons framework should be cascaded throughout the organisation so that every manager focuses on the short-, medium- and long-term development of their business unit. The authors claim to have demonstrated the effectiveness of the three Horizons framework by studying 30 high-growth companies in various industries and geographical territories.

At the time of writing some of these companies are still regarded as successful, for example, SAP, Walt Disney, Johnson & Johnson, Charles Schwab and GE Capital. Others however have not fared so well. Nokia has found it difficult to compete against Apple and Samsung and has now been acquired by Microsoft. Compaq struggled to compete with Dell's

94 *Strategic innovation management*

innovative business model and has been acquired by HP, itself a company struggling with growth. The lesson perhaps is that there is no 'silver bullet' model or framework that guarantees sustained growth in today's hypercompetitive global markets that are characterised by high levels of change, risk and uncertainty.

Nevertheless, the central idea of managing a portfolio of innovation projects across different timeframes is an enduring one and has been developed over time. Practical insights into how to manage the three Horizons include:

- Ensure the organisation establishes clear boundaries between each Horizon to ensure the performance of emerging Horizon 2 businesses are not measured against mature Horizon 1 businesses.
- Consider acquisitions in the short term to help fill the Horizon 2 portfolio. This is a quick and often cost-effective way of developing new growth opportunities.
- Focus on developing whole new businesses, not just new products, to improve the chances of commercial success.
- Focus on dominating a niche market where the new Horizon 2 business solves a mission-critical problem and can quickly build its market share, profits and brand.
- Leadership, not finance, is the most important and scarcest resource for developing Horizon 2 businesses. Ensure the organisation properly recognises and rewards Horizon 2 leaders to attract experienced and entrepreneurial leaders.

Ultimately the strength of the Horizons concept rests on the notion of managing innovation portfolios strategically over different timeframes and forcing managers to confront a painful truth: The current core business of the firm has a finite life and will eventually die. A strategic approach is therefore required to explore, nurture and develop the products and services that will become the future core business of the firm and underpin growth and success.

Innovation strategy and product life cycle

Products (and by extension technologies) have their own distinct life cycle, typically presented as a plot of annual market revenues against time. At the start of the product life cycle a new technology fights for market acceptance before (hopefully) experiencing a growth phase, then maturity, decline and finally obsolescence as it is replaced by another technology that offers the market greater utility (which could be superior functionality, lower price or both).

Strategic innovation management

Managing product life cycles strategically presents a significant challenge to organisations. For example, the capabilities required to develop and launch a new product are much different than those required to maintain high sales in a mature market. And how do you effectively manage a declining market while ensuring you are devoting sufficient resources to developing your own replacement technology?

These issues have been considered by Geoff Moore, an innovation consultant based in Silicon Valley, who has had ample opportunity to observe the birth, rise and fall of many products, technologies and even companies. In Moore's view, strategic investment in innovation has four potential returns:

Differentiation

Innovation that delivers differentiation in the marketplace allows the organisation to gain market share and charge higher prices than competitors.

Neutralisation

Innovation that delivers neutralisation allows the organisation to catch up with a competitor's differentiated offering or meet a new market Standard, thereby protecting market share.

Productivity

Innovation that delivers an increase in productivity reduces the organisation's costs, enabling it to achieve higher profit margins or higher market share by reducing prices. It can also free up resources that can then be redeployed to support differentiation or neutralisation programmes.

Waste

Some differentiation, neutralisation and productivity innovation programmes will not succeed. This is never a good result, but some failure is to be expected because there is no such thing as risk-free innovation. However, Moore classifies as 'waste' innovation programmes that go beyond what is required to succeed, yet the additional investment yields no further returns. Similarly, waste includes innovation programmes that achieve their stated objectives, but these are not enough to achieve a return; they were simply not ambitious enough.

Moore's great insight is that companies should carefully align their innovation strategy to fit specific segments of the life cycle, which are in turn aligned to the specific needs of the customer types. Moore proposes eight distinct phases within the life cycle:

1 Early market

This is where a new technology is first introduced to the market. The first customers who are attracted are themselves 'innovators', followed by 'early adopters', but the technology is still perceived as risky by the rest of the market. During this phase, companies entering the market are best served with a 'Disruptive Innovation' strategy that focuses on further developing the technology.

2 The chasm

The technology has now been in the market for some time and has lost some of its novelty. However, its acceptance is not yet widespread, and it still has not convinced the 'early majority' to adopt. To jump the 'chasm' across to the main market firms tend to focus on serving a very specific market niche, where the technology is the sole solution to a particular problem. As mentioned in Chapter 7 the classic example is the transistor, a technology which found a niche in portable radios.

3 Bowling alley

The technology is successful in its niche and now begins to be accepted in adjacent niches (hence the bowling alley metaphor), where it builds up a loyal following. Vendors utilise an 'application innovation' strategy to identify and explore applications in additional market niches.

4 Tornado

The technology has now gained wider acceptance and is seen as necessary for many applications, heralding a short period of intensive growth. New companies enter the market, and revenue growth is double or even triple digit, attracting additional investors. Firms focus on a 'product innovation' strategy, where the aim is to steadily improve the functionality and performance of the technology.

5 Main street (early)

Intensive growth has started to transition into a new phase of steady, long-term growth as markets expand. Market leaders have emerged, although

Strategic innovation management 97

smaller companies are still performing well as the 'early majority' starts to adopt the technology. Firms now focus on a 'process innovation' strategy to streamline production, the supply chain and order-fulfilment processes.

6 Main street (mature)

Growth in the market has now plateaued as the technology is increasingly seen as a commodity, though still useful. The market consolidates through mergers and acquisitions and the 'late majority' start to adopt the technology. Firms now focus on 'experiential innovation' and 'marketing innovation' strategies. These improve customer's experience of using the technology and improve marketing communications and customer touch points.

7 Main street (declining)

The technology is now fully commoditised, and some customers are actively looking for alternatives. The market is in need of disruption, and a next generation of technology is on the horizon. Nevertheless, the declining market is still profitable, and finally the 'laggards' are now adopting. Firms focus on a 'business model innovation' strategy to reframe the value proposition for customers. An example of this would be moving from a product purchase and service model to an all-inclusive leasing model.

8 Fault line and end of life

The technology is now obsolete, with a clear 'fault line' between what the market now wants and what the technology delivers. The next generation of technology is now being adopted, disrupting established vendors. There is no long-term future for vendors that only produce an obsolete technology, although there may be a few laggards willing to continue buying at rock-bottom prices. Firms now focus on a 'structural innovation' strategy to completely reposition themselves in the market. An example would be IBM, who when facing bankruptcy in the 1990s repositioned from an IT hardware supplier to a professional services provider.

Of course, you may reasonably argue that if a company has allowed itself to progress all the way to the 'end of life' without any back-up plan other than 'structural innovation' then it hasn't done a particularly good job at managing itself strategically. For example, it could have improved its situation by having a portfolio of different technologies at different points in the life cycle. But this approach depends on being able to redeploy resource from the day-to-day profit-generating activities that support a mature market to risky and speculative front-end innovation. This is often a tricky thing to do, as explored in the earlier section on Horizons.

First Mover Advantages

The decision on whether to be a technology leader or technology follower is a major strategic consideration. Being the first to bring a new innovative technology, product or service to market can generate significant competitive advantages, for example, by allowing the pioneering company to build up sales, market share and brand equity before followers enter the market. Once these advantages have been established the pioneer can enjoy a dominant position as the followers struggle to play catch-up—a 'First Mover Advantage'.

However, history shows that utilising a First Mover strategy does not guarantee success, and in fact a 'Fast Follower' strategy can often prove more effective. For example, pioneers like Ford, Intel and Rolls-Royce have continued to enjoy First Mover Advantages in the affordable automobile, microprocessor and gas turbine markets respectively. However, De Havilland, IBM and Raytheon failed to maintain their First Mover Advantage in the commercial jet, smartphone and microwave markets. It can therefore be seen that there are both First Mover Advantages and First Mover Disadvantages, and therefore 'market entry timing' is one of the key strategic decisions firms must make.

The academic study of First Mover Advantages can be traced back to the 1950s. However, interest in the area was spurred by Stanford Professors Marvin Lieberman and David Montgomery with the publication of their influential 1988 paper 'First Mover Advantages' in the prestigious *Strategic Management Journal*. This established many of the frameworks that have been subsequently explored by innovation, strategy and marketing scholars. Lieberman and Montgomery define First Mover Advantage simply as:

The ability of pioneering firms to earn positive economic profits.

There are three broad mechanisms that can lead to a First Mover Advantage: technological leadership, pre-emption of scarce assets and buyer switching costs.

Technological leadership

First Movers can gain advantage through technological leadership, which can be achieved by investments in R&D, joint ventures or acquisitions. Technological leadership generates an advantage in two ways: the 'learning curve' and patents.

Firstly, a cost advantage can be achieved through the 'learning curve' (sometimes referred to as the 'experience curve'). The learning curve model predicts that unit production costs fall as cumulative output increases due to learning (and experience) leading to improvements in efficiency. This in turn generates a sustainable cost advantage for the pioneering firm if learning can be kept proprietary. A cost advantage allows the pioneering firm to offer customers lower prices, therefore maintaining their attractiveness in the market compared to higher-priced new entrants.

Secondly, a pioneering firm with technological leadership can maintain an advantage over new entrants if the technology (or intellectual property) can be protected through patents. These prevent new entrants from reverse engineering and then copying the pioneer's technology for their own products. The pioneer will therefore retain their advantage until the patent expires, which is usually after 20 years. Ownership of technology-based intellectual property will form a central strategic consideration in whether to develop internal capabilities or to acquire from external sources.

Pre-emption of scarce assets

First Movers can gain advantage through the acquisition of scarce assets before their rivals, thus generating a sustainable advantage. These assets fall into two broad categories: input factors and spatial assets.

Input factors can include a wide range of assets, including natural resources (for example, rare earth metals), skilled labour, plant, manufacturing equipment and prime retailing locations. Input factors may also include access to external sources of knowledge and capabilities. By pre-empting rivals in securing these types of input factors an advantage over would-be followers can be achieved, hopefully deterring new entrants.

Spatial Assets are important in markets where there is only room for a limited number of profitable firms, so the First Mover can occupy an attractive position and deter new entrants. Space can be considered in terms of geographic location, the degree of market specialisation or factors such as limited retailing shelf space for certain product categories. For example, if you want to introduce a new brand of breakfast cereal, you will need to persuade retailers that they should reduce the amount of Kellogg's Cornflakes they stock—not an easy task.

Buyer switching costs

First Movers can gain an advantage by establishing high buyer switching costs, making it less likely that the buyer will drop the First Mover for a new entrant. Switching costs can broadly be categorised as transactional costs, learning costs, contractual costs and psychological costs.

Transactional Costs are related to the investment a buyer must initially make before changing supplier, including negotiations, performing credit checks, product trials and tests and retraining staff to use the new product.

Learning Costs are incurred when the buyer adapts to the characteristics of the product over time and therefore is reluctant to change. For example, a lecturer who has built their courses around a specific textbook will be reluctant to use a new textbook (even if it is superior and/or cheaper) because they will have to rewrite and re-plan all their lectures.

Contractual Costs are incurred when the supplier has either directly or indirectly built in contractual costs to changing suppliers. An example of a direct contractual cost would be an exclusivity clause for an agreed period of time. An example of an indirect contractual cost would be loyalty card schemes, such as frequent flyer programmes that make buyers reluctant to switch suppliers.

Psychological Costs are related to the reluctance of buyers to change suppliers due to the risk and uncertainty involved. First Movers can build up psychological costs by developing their positive brand attributes, such as quality, reliability, value for money and excellent customer service. For many years IBM salesmen would play on this, closing deals by looking the customer in the eye and saying, *"Nobody ever got fired for buying IBM!"*

First Mover Disadvantages

Lieberman and Montgomery also considered the factors that can cause First Mover Disadvantages. They propose four primary mechanisms: free-rider effects, technological and market uncertainty, shifts in technology or customer needs and incumbent inertia.

Free-rider effects are said to occur when new entrants benefit from the pioneer's investment in areas such as technology development, infrastructure development, market development and buyer education, thereby reducing their own costs and development time. For example, late entrants to the electric car market will benefit from increased consumer acceptance and the establishment of a network of recharging points.

Technological and market uncertainty are major risks associated with product launches. It is the First Movers who must accept these risks prior to launch. Fast Followers can gain an edge by adopting a 'wait and see' strategy and either delay entry until problems are resolved or decline to enter at all if problems are significant—in both cases saving a considerable amount of their own time and money.

Shifts in technology or customer needs can make a First Mover's offering obsolete, leaving the 'wait and see' followers in the prime position to capitalise on these shifts.

Incumbent inertia occurs when the First Mover becomes locked into focusing on their existing offering due to organisational inflexibility, reluctance to cannibalise existing product lines or reluctance to invest in new technologies and plants. These factors inhibit the ability of the firm to respond to new environmental or competitive threats, such as shifts in technology or customer needs.

First Mover Advantage theoretical limitations

So, given that there are both advantages and disadvantages, and many examples of winners and losers, how useful is the concept of First Mover Advantage to practicing managers? There are certainly limitations to the concept, and in today's fast-moving and globalised economy can there ever be a definitive classification of what a First Mover actually is? For example, if a firm enters an established market but with a new technology, should it be classified as a First Mover? What is the minimum size and duration of a First Mover's market share before it is considered a 'winner'? And is profit a better measure of success than market share? And even the three 'winners' given in the introduction as pioneers in their markets are today experiencing significant competition and reduced market share. In my view, the strength of the First Mover Advantage concept is that it forces firms to actively consider how innovation integrates with the wider business and commercial strategy of the firm. This in turn influences how the firm strategically invests in innovation resources and capabilities.

Innovation and entrepreneurship in action: Procter & Gamble

Procter & Gamble (P&G) is a global giant operating in the consumer goods market. Founded in Cincinnati in 1837 the company is now a billion-dollar enterprise best known for its portfolio of popular brands that include household names, such as Crest toothpaste, Head & Shoulders shampoo, Fairy washing up liquid, Ariel detergent and Olay skin care. Investment in R&D and consumer insights has traditionally underpinned P&G's approach to product and brand development, but a profits warning in 2000 and the appointment of A.G. Lafley as the new CEO became the catalyst for radically transforming innovation within the business.

Innovation had always been of strategic importance to P&G. Firstly, investors expect and demand consistent growth and dividend returns. While acquisitions can play a part, it is organic growth that is required to drive this, and as the company grew the R&D investment required became more and more difficult to maintain. Secondly, competition from both established firms, such as Unilever, and smaller entrepreneurial companies was becoming more intense. Thirdly, companies like P&G must convince supermarkets to stock their brands and then persuade consumers to pay a price premium compared to supermarkets' own brands. Bringing a steady stream of new, innovative and premium products successfully to market is therefore critical to P&G.

At the time, P&G was spending around $2 billion on R&D and a further $400 million on consumer insights, both significantly higher than industry benchmarks. P&G had well-established research facilities and around 7,500 scientists and technologists with expertise in chemistry, biology and life sciences. Yet, according to Lafley, only around 15% of innovations were meeting revenue and profit targets. The situation was unsustainable, and Lafley challenged his senior managers to come up with an innovation model that was more efficient, effective, repeatable and ultimately would deliver a sustainable competitive advantage.

Implementing change in a large and complex organisation such as P&G is inherently difficult. It was therefore essential that the drive was personally championed by Lafley to provide the visibility and impetus to the organisation. As Lafley noted, "*the Chief Executive Officer needs to be the Chief Innovation Officer!*" It was also important to experiment with a variety of approaches and then consolidate and integrate the most promising of these within the business. P&G worked with Harvard Professor Clayton Christensen to develop a framework that would allow innovation projects to be classified into one of four categories.

The first category was 'Sustaining Innovations' that deliver small, low-risk, incremental improvements to existing products, for example, longer-lasting detergent, better-tasting toothpaste and better-smelling shampoo. Sustaining Innovations are vital to protecting existing market share while also attracting new customers to try a product for the first time. The second category, 'Commercial Innovations', also drive sales of existing products, but rather than focusing on product improvement they utilise creative marketing, novel packaging and promotional tools to achieve this. The third category, 'Transformational-Sustaining Innovations', are higher risk but can bring significant benefits, for example, by reframing an existing category. Finally, 'Disruptive Innovations' are where a brand-new product, category or market is developed with a radically differentiated offering. These are the highest risk but can deliver the greatest benefits.

Developing a portfolio approach that manages risk across a range of innovation projects has been key to P&G's strategy. Simultaneously P&G

has considered organisational and structural factors. For example, they developed an innovation training programme, process manual and in-house advisors to support innovation projects. Opportunities to experiment, trial and develop new innovations were supported by the generation of small, entrepreneurial, multi-disciplinary teams. These were further developed into larger new-business creation groups and ultimately a full-scale 'innovation factory'. Importantly, strong links were developed with the core business units in order to benefit from their expertise in scale-up and project management disciplines.

Perhaps the most important development was the adoption of an Open Innovation approach to expand the opportunities for innovation far beyond the boundaries of the organisation. P&G estimated that for every researcher they employed there were approximately 200 scientists and engineers outside of P&G who may have solutions to scientific challenges and provide access to new opportunities. P&G launched the 'Connect and Develop' programme to tap into this external resource, reaching out to independent researchers, entrepreneurial companies, universities, suppliers and even retired scientists. To focus the organisation Lafley set an ambitious strategic target that 50% of new products should originate from external innovation. P&G also worked hard on adapting their culture from 'Not-Invented-Here' to 'Proudly-Found-Elsewhere'.

The effort to place innovation at the core of P&G's strategy appears to have paid off. Now 50% of innovations are delivering revenue and profit targets, up from 15%. This has been achieved without increasing R&D spend as a percentage of sales and has contributed to a significant rise in P&G's revenues, profits and share price.

Discussion and reflection activity

1 How could your organisation develop a portfolio of innovation projects within the three Horizons?
2 What is your organisation investing in innovation, and what are the expected returns?
3 What types of innovation should you apply to align with your product life cycle?
4 Is your organisation a First Mover or a Fast Follower, and what are the strategic implications?
5 Why is innovation strategically important to Procter & Gamble? What about for your organisation?
6 What aspects of Proctor & Gamble's innovation strategy could your organisation adopt?

Recommended reading

Brown, B. and Anthony, S. (2011). How P&G Tripled Its Innovation Success Rate. *Harvard Business Review*, 89(6), 64–72.

Keupp, M. M., Palmie, M. and Gassmann, O. (2012). The Strategic Management of Innovation: A Systematic Review and Paths for Future Research. *International Journal of Management Reviews*, 14(4), 367–390.

Kim, W. C. and Mauborgne, R. (2004). Value Innovation. *Harvard Business Review*, 82(7/8), 172–180.

Kim, W. C. and Mauborgne, R. (2019). Nondisruptive Creation: Rethinking Innovation and Growth. *MIT Sloan Management Review*, 60(3), 46–55.

Lieberman, M. and Montgomery, D. (1988a). First Mover Advantages. *Strategic Management Journal*, 9, 41–58.

Lieberman, M. and Montgomery, D. (1998b). First Mover (Dis)Advantages: Retrospective and Link with the Resource Based View. *Strategic Management Journal*, 19(12), 1111–1125.

Moore, G. (2004). Darwin and the Demon: Innovating Within Established Enterprises. *Harvard Business Review*, 82(7/8), 86–92.

Moore, G. (2006). *Dealing with Darwin: How Great Companies Innovate at Every Phase of Their Evolution*. Chichester: Wiley.

Moore, G. (2007). To Succeed in the Long Term, Focus on the Middle Term. *Harvard Business Review*, 85(7), 84–90.

Nagji, B. and Tuff, G. (2012). Managing Your Innovation Portfolio. *Harvard Business Review*, 90(5), 66–74.

Pisano, G. P. (2015). You Need an Innovation Strategy. *Harvard Business Review*, 93(6), 44–54.

Postner, B. and Mangelsdorf, M. (2017). 12 Essential Innovation Insights. *MIT Sloan Management Review*, 59(1), 28–36.

Song, M., Zhao, L. and Di Benedetto, A. C. (2013). Do Perceived Pioneering Advantages Lead to First-Mover Decisions? *Journal of Business Research*, 66(8), 1143–1152.

Suarez, F. and Lanzolla, G. (2005). The Half Truth of First Mover Advantage. *Harvard Business Review*, 83(4), 121–127.

Zachary, M. A., Gianiodis, P. T., Payne, G. T. and Markman, G. D. (2015). Entry Timing: Enduring Lessons and Future Directions. *Journal of Management*, 41(5), 1388–1415.

Further reading

Congratulations on reaching the end of the book! I hope the topics covered provide a solid introduction to the subject area and also generate interest in further developing your understanding of the field. Some additional, contemporary and emerging areas of innovation and entrepreneurship research and practice which could not be covered within the scope of the eight chapters are highlighted here:

Innovation and sustainability

Adams, R., Jeanrenaud, S., Bessant, J., Denyer, D. and Overy, P. (2016). Sustainability-Oriented Innovation: A Systematic Review. *International Journal of Management Reviews*, 18(1), 180–205.

Geradts, T. and Bocken, N. (2019). Driving Sustainability-Orientated Innovation. *MIT Sloan Management Review*, 60(2), 1–9.

Jin, Z., Navare, J. and Lynch, R (2019). The Relationship Between Innovation Culture and Innovation Outcomes: Exploring the Effects of Sustainability Orientation and Firm Size. *R&D Management*, 49(4), 607–623.

Lampikoski, T., Westerlund, M., Rajala, R. and Moller, K. (2014). Green Innovation Games: Value Creation Strategies for Corporate Sustainability. *California Management Review*, 57(1), 88–116.

Varadarajan, R. (2017). Innovating for Sustainability: A Framework for Sustainable Innovations and a Model of Sustainable Innovations Orientation. *Journal of the Academy of Marketing Science*, 45(1), 14–36.

Voegtlin, C. and Scherer, A. (2017). Responsible Innovation and the Innovation of Responsibility: Governing Sustainable Development in a Globalized World. *Journal of Business Ethics*, 143(2), 227–243.

Design thinking

Brown, T. (2008). Design Thinking. *Harvard Business Review*, 86(6), 84–82.

Elsbach, K. and Stigliani, I. (2018). Design Thinking and Organizational Culture: A Review and Framework for Future Research. *Journal of Management*, 44(6), 2274–2306.

Further reading

Knight, E., Daymond, J. and Paroutis, S. (2020). Design-Led Strategy: How to Bring Design Thinking into the Art of Strategic Management. *California Management Review*, 62(2), 30–52.

Liedtka, J. (2018). Why Design Thinking Works. *Harvard Business Review*, 96(5), 72–79.

Mahmoud-Jouini, Sihem, B., Fixson, S. and Boulet, D. (2019). Making Design Thinking Work: Adapting an Innovation Approach to Fit a Large Technology-Driven Firm. *Research Technology Management*, 62(5), 50–58.

Nakata, C. (2020). Design Thinking for Innovation: Considering Distinctions, Fit, and Use in Firms. *Business Horizons*, 63(6), 763–772.

Business model innovation

Christensen, C. M., Bartman, T. and van Bever, D. (2016). The Hard Truth About Business Model Innovation. *MIT Sloan Management Review*, 53(3), 30–40.

Foss, N. and Saebi, T. (2017). Fifteen Years of Research on Business Model Innovation: How Far Have We Come, and Where Should We Go? *Journal of Management*, 43(1), 200–227.

Markides, C. (2013). Business Model Innovation: What Can the Ambidexterity Literature Teach Us? *Academy of Management Perspectives*, 27(4), 313–323.

Osterwalder, A. and Pigneur, Y. (2010). *Business Model Generation*. Hoboken, NJ: John Wiley & Sons.

Taran, Y., Bo, H. and Lindgren, P. (2015). A Business Model Innovation Typology. *Decision Sciences*, 46(2), 301–331.

Teece, D. (2010). Business Models, Business Strategy and Innovation. *Long Range Planning*, 43(2), 172–194.

Digital innovation

Fitzgerald, M., Kruschwitz, N., Bonnet, D. and Welch, M. (2013). Embracing Digital Technology: A New Strategic Imperative. *MIT Sloan Management Review*, 1–12.

Hagiu, A. and Wright, J. (2020). When Data Creates Competitive Advantage. *Harvard Business Review*, 98(1), 94–101.

Iansiti, M. and Lakhani, K. (2020). Competing in the Age of AI. *Harvard Business Review*, 98(1), 60–67.

Kohli, R. and Melville, N. P. (2019). Digital Innovation: A Review and Synthesis. *Information Systems Journal*, 29(1), 200–223.

Nambsian, S., Lyytinen, K., Majchrzak, A. and Song, M. (2017). Digital Innovation Management: Reinventing Innovation Management in a Digital World. *MIS Quarterly*, 41(1), 223–238.

Nambisan, S., Wright, M. and Feldman, M. (2019). The Digital Transformation of Innovation and Entrepreneurship: Progress, Challenges and Key Themes. *Research Policy*, 48(8). https://doi.org/10.1016/j.respol.2019.03.018.

Entrepreneurship and diversity

Adachi, T. and Hisada, T. (2017). Gender Differences in Entrepreneurship and Intrapreneurship: An Empirical Analysis. *Small Business Economics*, 48, 447–486.

Dean, H., Larsen, G., Ford, J. and Akram, M. (2019). Female Entrepreneurship and the Metanarrative of Economic Growth. *International Journal of Management Reviews*, 21(1), 24–49.

Gonzalez-Pernia, J., Jung, A. and Pena, I. (2015). Innovation-Driven Entrepreneurship in Developing Economies. *Entrepreneurship and Regional Development*, 27(9/10), 555–573.

Harrison, R., Leitch, C. and McAdam, M. (2015). Breaking Glass: Toward a Gendered Analysis of Entrepreneurial Leadership. *Journal of Small Business Management*, 53, 693–713.

Hughs, K., Jennings, J., Brush, C., Carter, S. and Welter, F. (2012). Extending Women's Entrepreneurship Research in New Directions. *Entrepreneurship Theory and Practice*, 36, 429–442.

Ram, M., Jones, T. and Villares—Varela, M. (2017). Migrant Entrepreneurship: Reflections on Research and Practice. *International Small Business Journal*, 35(1), 3–18.

Social entrepreneurship

Andre, K. and Pache, A. C. (2016). From Caring Entrepreneur to Caring Enterprise: Addressing the Ethical Challenge of Scaling up Social Enterprises. *Journal of Business Ethics*, 133(4), 659–675.

Clark, K. D., Newbert, S. L. and Quigley, N. R. (2018). The Motivational Drivers Underlying For-Profit Venture Creation: Comparing Social and Commercial Entrepreneurs. *International Small Business Journal*, 36(2), 220–241.

Gupta, P., Chauhan, S., Paul, J. and Jaiswal, M. (2020). Social Entrepreneurship Research: A Review and Future Research Agenda. *Journal of Business Research*, 113, 209–229.

Hlady-Rispal, M. and Servantie, V. (2018). Deconstructing the way in which Value is Created in the Context of Social Entrepreneurship. *International Journal of Management Reviews*, 20(1), 62–80.

Mair, J., Battilana, J., Cardenas, J. (2012). Organising for Society: A Typology of Social Entrepreneurship Models. *Journal of Business Ethics*, 111(3), 353–373.

Stevens, R., Moray, N. and Bruneel, J. (2015). The Social and Economic Mission of Social Enterprises: Dimensions, Measurement, Validation and Relation. *Entrepreneurship Theory and Practice*, 39(5), 1051–1082.

Index

Note: Page numbers in *italics* indicate a figure on the corresponding page.

3Com 75
3M 49–50

Abernathy, Bill 86
absorptive capacity 63–64, 71, 72–73
adoption of innovations 71, 72
Allen, Thomas 71, 73
angel investors 26, 29
Anthony, Scott 2, 75
Apex Ltd 88
Apple 5, 20–22, 40–43, 73–74, 81, 93
application innovation 96
associating 9

Baghai, Mehrdad 92
Bailey, Pete 36
BBC's *Dragons' Den* programme 29
Betamax video system 86
biotechnology 17, 67
Birch, David 1, 6–7
blue sky research 56
Blu-Ray system 86
Bohr, Niels 85
Bower, Joseph 79
bowling alley 96
brand equity 98
brand management 46
bricolage 26, 30–31
Burns, Ursula 75
business life cycle 92
business model innovation 75, 97, 106
business plan 27, 30
business strategy, for growth 14, 68

buyer education 100
buyer switching costs 91, 98, 99–100

cannibalising existing product lines, threat of 32
Cantillon, Richard 3
causation 30–31
changes in perception 13, 14, 17
chasm 96
Chesbrough, Henry 63, 67–68, 71
Christensen, Clayton 75, 78, 79–81, 102
Cisco Systems 81
Clagett, Robert 71
clusters *see* industrial 'clusters'
codification 52, 54–55
Cohen, Wesley 72
Cold War 22
Coley, Stephen 92
collaboration 43, 54, 60–61, 68–69
collaborative innovation 63
Collington, Russ 36
Commercial Innovations 102
compact disc technology 84
competency development 32–33
competition, for budgets and resources 8
competitive advantage 14, 21, 31, 47, 53, 55–56, 98, 102
Competitive Advantage of Nations, The (1990) 21
conflict-avoidance 19
contextual ambidexterity 40, 44, 45–46
contractual costs 100

copyright 64–65
corporate entrepreneurship 4
corporate strategy 54
corporate venture capital (CVC) 27, 34
corporate venturing 27; to build leadership capability 35; capture knowledge and learning 36; commitment for 35; to establish realistic expectations 35; Fortune 500 companies 34; managing with a portfolio mindset 35–36; new venture creation via 33–36; portfolio of 35; strategic impact of 34–36; types of 34
creative destruction 1, 4–6, 75
creative solutions, development of 18
creativity: fostering 18–20; group 19; individual 18–19; left brain/right brain theory of 18; notion of 13; organisational 19–20; pitfalls of 20; reasons for 18
crowdfunding 26, 30, 37–38
Cugnot, Nicholas-Joseph 87

Daimler Motor Company 87
data collection 9–10
decision-making 8, 20, 31, 64, 71
delayed switching 83–84
Dell, Michael 10
demographic changes 13, 14, 16
design thinking 105
diamond model 14
differentiation 95
Digital Equipment Corporation (DEC) 74
digital innovation 106
digital photography 81
digital technologies 44
discovery skills 9, 10
Disruptive Innovations 79–81, 96, 102; adoption of 80; defined 78–79; Ford Model T 80; responsibility for developing 81; *versus* sustaining innovation 79–80
disruptive technologies 34, 79, 81
diversity 33, 57, 107
dominant design 79, 86–87
Dragons Den 3
Drew, Dick 49–50

Drucker, Peter 4, 13–14, 18; knowledge economy 53; on sources of opportunity for organisations and entrepreneurs 14; view of innovation 14
dual cyclone technology 87–88
due diligence 30, 67
Duncan, Robert 43
Dvorak, August 85
Dvorak Simplified Keyboard (DSK) 85
Dyson, James 3, 66, 87–88

early adopters 96
early majority 96, 97
early market 96
economic development 52, 55–57
economic impact, of innovation and entrepreneurship: 'elephants, mice and gazelles' model 6–7; government policy, implications for 7–8; large organisations, implications for 8–9
economics of the industry 15
economies of scale 55, 86
Edison, Thomas 14
effectuation 30–31
electric and petrol-powered automobiles 87
electric car market 100
elephant firms 6, 8, 9, 35
elephants, mice and gazelles, Birch's notion of 6–7
emerging economies 53
emerging technology 83
'Empire Strikes Back, The' (2012) 75–76
employee recruitment 72
employment, private-sector 6
employment security, based on the skills and mobility 7
end of life 97–98
entreprende 3
entrepreneurial behaviour 9
entrepreneurial firms 5, 18, 26
Entrepreneurial University 52, 56–58
entrepreneurs: defined 1; innovative capabilities of 31; problem-solving ability 13, 18–19, 31; Schumpeter's view of 4–6
entrepreneurship: in action 9–10; definitions of 3–4; impact

on economic growth 1, 6–9; Schumpeterian perspectives on 4–6
equity funding 67
E. Remington & Sons 85
Ethernet 74–75
Etzkowitz, Henry 52, 55–57
Evans, Hugh 36–37
experience curve 99
experiential innovation 97
experimenting, concept of 10
expertise 18
explicit knowledge 53
exploitation 2, 40, 43–46
exploration 2, 19, 40, 43–46
external corporate venturing (ECV) 27, 34
extrinsic motivation 18–19

Facebook 5, 20–21, 37, 59
face-to-face communication 55
false negatives *see* type II errors
false positives *see* type I errors
family, friends (and fools) 26, 28
Fast Follower 98
fault line 97–98
financial markets, deregulation of 16
firm competitiveness 21
First Mover Advantage strategy 86, 91, 98–100; buyer switching costs 99–100; classification of 101; concept of 101; pre-emption of scarce assets 99; technological leadership 98–99; theoretical limitations 101
First Mover Disadvantages 92, 98; free-rider effects 100; incumbent inertia 101; shifts in technology or customer needs 101; technological and market uncertainty 100
five forces model 21
Ford, Henry 42, 58, 80
Ford Model T 80
Ford Motor Company 87, 98
Fortune 500 companies 3, 14, 34
free revealing 59
free-rider effects 100
frequent flyer programmes 100
fuel economy 82, 84
funding options, for start-ups 26, 27–30; angel investors 29; business plan 27; crowdfunding 30; from family and friends 28; grants 27–28; levels of 27; loans 28–29; personal savings 28; venture capitalists 29–30

Gates, Bill 81
gazelle firms: challenge for 8–9; growth of 7, 8; Research and Development (R&D) 14, 20
General Electric (GE) 6, 41, 46
General Motors 41, 47, 87
generating ideas, process for 13, 14–17
G-Force 88
goals, achievement of 9
good management practice 78, 80
Gore-Tex 23
Gore, Wilbert Lee 'Bill' 23–24
government agencies 28
grants 27–28
graphene 17
greenhouse gas emissions 87
group creativity 19
groupthink 19

halo effect 10
Haloid Photographic Company *see* Xerox
Hamel, Gary 46–47
Heffalump 3
high-growth firms: causation, effectuation and bricolage 30–31; choice of market scope 32; competency development 32–33; management of resources 30–33; market-leading position 31; risk and radical innovation 31–33; role of leaders, teams and networks 33
high-technology companies 20, 22
Hoover 66, 88
Horizons: developing innovation 92–94; first mover advantages 91; first mover disadvantages 92; Horizon 1 91, 92; Horizon 2 91, 92–93; Horizon 3 93–94; innovation strategy 94–95; product life cycle 94–95; three Horizons of growth 91
human knowledge 56

IBM 75, 81, 97–98, 100
ideas and opportunities, process for generating 14–17

incongruities 13, 14, 15–16
incremental innovations 26, 31–32
incumbent inertia 100–101
individual creativity 18–19
industrial clusters 14, 20–22
industrial districts 21
industry or market changes 13, 14, 16
in-field experimentation 58
information sharing 49, 55, 59
information technology (IT) 17, 54–55
infrastructure development 7, 100
initial public offerings (IPOs) 21, 29
Innocentive 70
innovare 2
innovation: in action 9–10; areas of technology leading to 17; defined 1, 2–3; Drucker's view on 14; impact on economic growth 1, 6–9; Mark I and Mark II models of 1, 4–6; Schumpeterian perspectives on 4–6
innovation factory 103
innovation management 79
innovation training programme 103
innovative products and services: development of 8; market for 17
Innovator's Dilemma, The 79
innovator's DNA 9–10
Instagram 37, 59
Intel 20, 27, 34–35, 74, 98
intellectual property 21, 27, 59; meaning of 64; methods of legally protecting 64–67; Open Innovation for management of 69; ownership of technology-based 99; patents for protection of 63, 65–67, 86; protection strategy 66
interest repayments 26
inter-firm rivalry 22
internal corporate venturing (ICV) 27, 34
intolerance to failure 13, 20
intrapreneurship 4
intrinsic motivation 19–20
intrinsic personality traits 9
iPhone 41–42, 46
Ive, Jonathan 42

job for life 7
job security 7, 72
Jobs, Steve 40–43, 74

joint ventures 45, 98
JVC 86

Katz, Ralph 71, 73
Kauffman Foundation 3
Kellogg's Cornflakes 99
Kickstarter 30
Kilby, Peter 3
knowledge: monopoly of 71; repository of 55; sources of 54
knowledge-driven organisational culture, development of 54
knowledge economy 53, 56
knowledge-focused projects 54
knowledge management: approaches for 52, 54; codification strategy 52, 54–55; defined 52, 53; explicit knowledge 53; innovation and strategy 53–54; mechanisms for 53; personalisation strategy 52, 54–55; tacit knowledge 53
knowledge workers 53
Kodak 6, 21, 44, 81
Kroc, Ray 15

labour force 7
labour markets 67
Lafley, A.G. 101–103
laggards 97
laser printer 74, 75
late majority 97
leadership insights, into developing and sustaining innovation: focus 41; high-performance environment 43; intuition 42; reinvention 42; simplicity 42
leadership, role of 33, 40
Lead Users 53, 58–59
learning costs 100
learning curve 91, 98–99
left brain/right brain theory, for creativity 18
Lego 59–60
Levinthal, Daniel 72
licencing 54, 65, 70
Lieberman, Marvin 98, 100
loans 28–29, 30, 56
locus of control 9

main street: declining 97; early 96–97; mature 97

management innovation 41, 46–49; analogies and exemplars from different environments 48; capabilities to remain competitive 48; capacity for low-risk experimentation 48–49; definition of 46; developing of 48–49; examples of 46–47; foundation of 47; key areas of 48–49; opportunities for 47–48; problem-solving culture 48; use of external change agents to explore new ideas 49
manufacturing-centred innovation 52, 58–59
March, James 43
market development 100
market entry timing 98
marketing innovation 97
market leaders 96
mark I model 1, 4–5
mark II model 1, 4, 5–6, 8
mature technology 84
McColough, Peter 73
McDonald's 15
McKinsey & Company 92
Merck 67
mergers and acquisitions 97–98
Metcalfe, Robert 74–75
mice 6–7
Microsoft 5, 59, 73, 74, 93
Minnesota Mining and Manufacturing Company *see* 3M
monopoly rights 66
Montgomery, David 98, 100
Moore, Geoff 95–96
motivation 13; extrinsic 18–19; intrinsic 19, 20

nationalised industries, privatisation of 16
need for achievement (nAch) 9
networking, significance of 10
networks, role of 33
neutralisation 95
new knowledge 13, 14, 17, 20, 45, 52, 54, 57
new products, development of 33
Newton, Isaac 65
NineSigma 70
Nobel Prize 18

not-for-profit agencies 28
Not-Invented-Here Syndrome (NIH Syndrome) 63–64, 68–69; academic study of 71; characteristics of 71–72; decision-making and 71; definition of 71; influence on absorptive capacity 73; Open Innovation and 71

observing 10
ocean shipping economics 16
Ofcom regulation 37
Olds Motor Vehicle Company 87
Open Innovation 63; barrier to implementing 72; business model 69; characteristics of 68–71; concept of 71; development of 67–68; implementation of 73; for intellectual property management 69; metrics used to measure 70–71
operational efficiency and execution 44
operational-level enthusiasm 33
organisational ambidexterity 43–46; contextual 40, 45–46; development of 45; structural 40, 44–45
organisational creativity 19–20
organisational deficiencies 48
organisational interfaces 73
organisational structure 20, 45, 47
Organisation for Economic Co-operation and Development (OECD) 2
outsourcing 7, 22, 45, 53

Palo Alto Research Centre (PARC) 73–74
parallel technology, development of 84
patents 46, 98–99; applications 66; disadvantages with 66; expensive and time consuming 66; industrial application 65–66; infringement of 66–67; inventiveness 65; novelty 65; portfolios of 67; for protection of intellectual property 63, 65–67; purpose of 63, 65
patent sharks 66–67
patent trolls 66–67
peer-to-peer lending 30
performance myopia 84–85
personalisation 52, 54–55
personality traits 9

Index

personal savings 26, 28
Pfizer 15
Pixar 43
Porter, Michael 14, 21
post-industrial knowledge economy 56
premature switching 83
Primordial Radio 36–38
problem-solving ability 13, 18–19, 31, 48, 73
process innovation 71, 97
process manual 103
process needs 13–14, 16
Procter & Gamble (P&G) 46, 101–103
product development 41, 59–60, 67, 87
product innovation 75, 96
productivity 95
product launches, risks associated with 8, 10, 100
product life cycle 91; bowling alley 96; the chasm 96; differentiation 95; early market 96; fault line and end of life 97–98; innovation strategy and 94–95; main street (declining) 97; main street (early) 96–97; main street (mature) 97; management of 95; neutralisation 95; phases within 96–98; productivity 95; tornado 96; waste 95–98
product performance 84
product-to-human interfaces 78–79, 87
project management 47, 103
psychological costs 100

questioning 10
QWERTY keyboard 74, 85, 87

radical innovation 26, 30–33
registered designs 64–65
Research and Development (R&D) 66, 82, 98; clusters and innovation 20–23; governmental perspective on 20; in-house 54, 56; investment in developing a technology 78, 83; return on investment 35; support to high-growth gazelle firms 14, 20
research-intensive companies 68
resource allocation 45
resource constraints 26, 30–31, 38
resources, management of 30–33
return on investment 35

reward and incentive schemes 72
risk: aversion, levels of 13; avoidance, levels of 8; components of 70; tolerance 9
risk-free innovation 95
risk-taking and investment 8
Rogers, Everett 2
Rolls-Royce 68, 98
Rosenzweig, Phil 10
royalty payments 67
Ryanair 5, 81

Say, Jean-Baptiste 4
scarce assets, pre-emption of 99
Schumpeter, Joseph 1, 4–6
scientific discoveries 20, 46
S-Curve model 78, *82*, 82–85
Seedrs 30, 37
self-esteem 9
senior sponsors, identification of 33
service-based businesses 27
Shaw, Percy 16
shipbuilding industry 15
Sholes, Christopher Latham 85
Silicon Valley 20–22, 73, 95
single-crystal blade technology 84
Sloan, Alfred P. 47
small to medium enterprises (SMEs) 44
social entrepreneurship 107
Sony 59, 86
Sperry, Roger 18
spin-off ventures 34
spin-out ventures 34
standard design 86
standards 36; technology 85–87; wars, between rival firms 79, 86
Starkweather, Gary 75
start-ups 8, 21, 67; founding entrepreneur 33; funding options for 27–30; lending money for 28; new venture formation 27; opportunities for innovation 31; venture capital-backed 35
strategic alliances 54, 94
Strategic Management Journal 98
strategy development 36
structural ambidexterity 40, 44–45
structural innovation 97
student loans 56
supply chain 97

sustainability 105
sustainable growth 93
sustaining innovation 102; defined 78–79; *versus* disruptive innovation 79–80

tacit knowledge 53, 55, 79, 87
teams, role of 33
technological competencies 54
technological discontinuities 82–85
technological factors 54
technological innovation 66–67, 82
technological leadership 91, 98–99
technological obsolescence 83
technological 'Standard' 78
technology: application of 17; commercialisation of 17, 35; development 75, 81, 83, 100; intermediaries 69–70; leading to the development of new innovations 17; standards 85–87
technology-driven markets 66
three Horizons of growth: Horizon 1 91, 92; Horizon 2 91, 92–93; Horizon 3 93–94
tornado 96
Toyota 41, 47
trademarks 64–65
trade-offs 32, 41, 43, 47
transactional costs 100
Transformational-Sustaining Innovations 102
trial-and-error type methodologies 58

Triple Helix Association 56
Triple Helix paradigm 52, 55–56
tuition fees 56
Twitter 37
type I errors 70
type II errors 70

uncertainty 32, 71, 92, 94, 100
unexpected occurrences 13, 14, 15
university education, demand for 56
user-centred innovation 52–53, 58–59
Utterback, James 86

value capture 68
value creation 68
venture capital funding 29–30, 37, 75
venture capitalists 21, 26, 29–30, 34
venture creation 33–36
Viagra 15
Video Home System (VHS) 86
von Hippel, Eric 52, 58, 68

waste 95–98
Western economies 53
White, David 92
WL Gore and Associates 22–24
Woodhouse, Ben 36

Xerox 73–75
Xerox Alto 74

youth unemployment 7